كلمة التوحيد

THE STATEMENT
OF AT-TAWHĪD:
Lā Ilaha Illā-Allāh
(ITS VIRTUES, SIGNIFICANCE,
CONDITIONS, & NULLIFIERS)

Shaykh 'Abdur-Razzāq Ibn 'Abdul-Muhsin al-'Abbād al-Badr

ISBN: 978-1-9438-4470-8

First Edition: Dhul Hijjah 1436 A.H. /October 2015 C.E.

Cover Design: Abū Sulaymān Muhammad 'Abdul-Azim Ibn Joshua Baker

Translation by Aboo Farooq Abdur Rahman 'Abdullah al-Yemeni

Revision made by Maktabatulirshad staff

Typesetting & formatting by Abū Sulaymān Muhammad 'Abdul-'Azim Ibn Joshua Baker

Printing: Ohio Printing

Subject: 'Aqīdah & Tawhīd

Website: www.maktabatulirshad.com
E-mail: info@maktabatulirshad.com

Contents

BRIEF BIOGRAPHY OF THE AUTHOR

His name: Shaykh 'Abdur-Razzāq Ibn 'Abdul-Muhsin al-'Abbād al-Badr.

He is the son of the *'Allāmah* and *Muhaddith* of Medina Shaykh 'Abdul-Muhsin al-'Abbād al-Badr.

Birth: He was born on the 22nd day of *Dhul-Qa'dah* in the year 1382 AH in az-Zal'fi, Kingdom of Saudi Arabia. He currently resides in Medina.

Current Occupation: He is a member of the teaching staff at the Islāmic University of Medina.

Scholastic Certifications: Doctorate in *'Aqīdah*.

The Shaykh has authored books, researches, as well as numerous explanations in different sciences. Among them are:

1. *Fiqh of Supplications & adh-Kār.*

2. *Hajj & Refinement of the Souls.*

3. Explanation of the book, E*xemplary Principles*, by Shaykh Ibn 'Uthaymīn (رَحِمَهُٱللَّهُ).

4. Explanation of the book, *The Principles of Names & Attributes*, authored by Shaykh-ul-Islām Ibn al-Qayyim (رَحِمَهُ ٱللَّهُ).

5. Explanation of the book, *Good Words*, authored by Shaykh-ul-Islām Ibn al-Qayyim (رَحِمَهُ ٱللَّهُ).

6. Explanation of the book, *al-Aqīdah at-Tahāwiyyah*.

7. Explanation of the book, *Fusūl: Biography of the Messenger*, by Ibn Kathīr (رَحِمَهُ ٱللَّهُ).

8. A full explanation of the book, *al-Adab-ul-Mufrad*, authored by Imam Bukhārī (رَحِمَهُ ٱللَّهُ).

From the most distinguished scholars whom he has taken and acquired knowledge from are:

1. His father the *'Allāmah* Shaykh 'Abdul-Muhsin al-Badr (حفظه الله).

2. The *'Allāmah* Shaykh Ibn Bāz (رَحِمَهُ ٱللَّهُ).

3. The *'Allāmah* Shaykh Muhammad Ibn Sālih al-'Uthaymīn (رَحِمَهُ ٱللَّهُ).

4. Shaykh 'Ali Ibn Nāsir al-Faqīhi (حفظه الله).

ARABIC SYMBOL TABLE

Arabic Symbols & their meanings

حفظه الله	May Allāh preserve him
رَضِّاَللَّهُعَنْهُ	(i.e. a male companion of the Prophet Muhammad)
سُبْحَانَهُوَتَعَالَى	Glorified & Exalted is Allāh
عَزَّوَجَلَّ	(Allāh) the Mighty & Sublime
تَبَارَكَوَتَعَالَى	(Allāh) the Blessed & Exalted
جَلَّوَعَلَا	(Allāh) the Sublime & Exalted
عَلَيْهِٱلصَّلَاةُوَٱلسَّلَامُ	May Allāh send Blessings & Safety upon him (i.e. a Prophet or Messenger)
صَلَّىٱللَّهُعَلَيْهِوَعَلَىآلِهِوَسَلَّمَ	May Allāh send Blessings & Safety upon him and his family (i.e. Du'ā send mentioned the Prophet Muhammad)
رَحِمَهُٱللَّهُ	May Allāh have mercy upon him
رَضِّاَللَّهُعَنْهُمْ	May Allāh be pleased with them (i.e. Du'ā made for the Companions of the Prophet Muhammad)
جَلَّجَلَالُهُ	(Allāh) His Majesty is Exalted
رَضِّاَللَّهُعَنْهَا	May Allāh be pleased with her (i.e. a female companion of the Prophet Muhammad)

INTRODUCTION

All praise is for Allāh the Lord of the worlds. I bear witness that there is no deity worthy of worship except Allāh alone with no partners, and I bear witness that Muhammad (ﷺ) is His slave and Messenger.

Thereafter, this treatise contains a beneficial summary of the best of words, and the greatest and most lofty: the word of *Tawhid* (لا إله إلا الله) – *none has the right to be worshiped in truth except Allāh* – its virtues, significance, conditions, and nullifiers. The treatise is extracted from my book *"Fiqh Al-Adiyah wal Adkaar."* It was requested by some of our noble acquaintances to isolate this treatise to a separate authoring for ease of benefit.

I pray to Allāh to place in this treatise a great blessing. May He make it a door of guidance for whom He wills of His servants. May He guide us all to His straight path; the path of those that Allāh favored amongst the Messengers, the truthful, martyrs, and the righteous, and how excellent these companions are. Allāh is sufficient for us, and He is the best disposer of affairs. May peace and blessings be upon our Prophet and his family.

Written by: 'Abdur-Razzāq al-Badr

VIRTUES OF THE STATEMENT: "NONE HAS THE RIGHT TO BE WORSHIPPED IN TRUTH BUT ALLĀH."

Indeed, to this splendid statement belong excellent virtues and innumerable distinctions. It is the best, most virtuous, and the greatest of all statements. For its cause, the creation was created, messengers sent, and books were revealed. By this declaration, mankind was separated into believers and disbelievers; joyous dwellers of paradise and wretched dwellers of Hellfire. So it is the most trustworthy handhold that will never break, the statement of piety, the greatest of all pillars of religion, and the largest of the branches of faith. Moreover, it is the path of attaining Paradise and salvation from the Fire. It is the statement of testimony, the key to the Home of Bliss, and salvation from the Hellfire. It is the foundation of the religion and the pinnacle of its matters.

The virtue of this statement and its lofty position in the religion is above what anyone could describe or fully grasp.

Allāh (سُبْحَانَهُوَتَعَالَ) said:

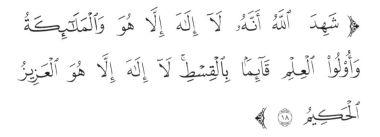

"Allāh bears witness that Lā Ilāha Illā
Huwa (none has the right to be worshipped but
He), and the angels, and those having knowledge
(also give this witness); (He always) maintains
His creation in Justice. Lā Ilāha Illā Huwa (none
has the right to be worshipped but He), the All-
Mighty, the All-Wise." [*Sūrah Āli Imran* 3:18]

From amongst the mentions of the virtues of this
statement in the Noble Qur'ān: Allāh (تَبَارَكَوَتَعَالَى) made it
the core call of the prophets and the essence of their
message. Allāh (سُبْحَانَهُوَتَعَالَى) says:

﴿ وَمَآ أَرْسَلْنَا مِن قَبْلِكَ مِن رَّسُولٍ إِلَّا نُوحِى إِلَيْهِ
أَنَّهُ لَآ إِلَهَ إِلَّا أَنَا۠ فَٱعْبُدُونِ ۝ ﴾

"And We did not send any Messenger before you
(O Muhammad صَلَّىاللَّهُعَلَيْهِوَسَلَّمَ) but We revealed to him
(saying): Lā Ilāha Illā Ana [none has the right to

be worshipped but I (Allāh)], so worship Me
(Alone and none else)." [*Sūrah al-Anbiyā'* 21:25]

And He (سُبْحَانَهُوَتَعَالَى) said:

﴿ وَلَقَدْ بَعَثْنَا فِي كُلِّ أُمَّةٍ رَّسُولًا أَنِ ٱعْبُدُواْ
ٱللَّهَ وَٱجْتَنِبُواْ ٱلطَّٰغُوتَ ﴾

"And verily, We have sent among
every Ummah (community, nation) a Messenger
(proclaiming): "Worship Allāh (Alone), and
avoid (or keep away from) *Tāghūt* (all false
deities i.e. do not worship Tāghūt besides
Allāh)." [*Sūrah an-Nahl* 16:36]

And He (سُبْحَانَهُوَتَعَالَى) said in the opening of the chapter Nahl:

﴿ يُنَزِّلُ ٱلْمَلَٰٓئِكَةَ بِٱلرُّوحِ مِنْ أَمْرِهِۦ عَلَىٰ مَن يَشَآءُ
مِنْ عِبَادِهِۦٓ أَنْ أَنذِرُوٓاْ أَنَّهُۥ لَآ إِلَٰهَ إِلَّآ أَنَا۠ فَٱتَّقُونِ

 ﴾

"He sends down the angels with the Rūh (revelation) of His Command to whom of His slaves He wills (saying): "Warn mankind that Lā Ilāha Illā Ana (none has the right to be worshipped in truth but I), so fear Me (by abstaining from sins and evil deeds)." [*Sūrah an-Nahl* 16:2]

This verse is the first of enumerated bounties of Allāh upon his servants, to indicate that the guidance to this statement is the greatest bounty that Allāh bestowed upon His slaves, As He (سُبْحَانَهُوَتَعَالَى) says:

"And has completed and perfected His Graces upon you, (both) apparent and hidden." [*Sūrah Luqmān* 31:20]

Mujāhid – (رَحِمَهُٱللَّه) - said:

"[the grace is] the statement of *Lā Ilaha Illā-Allāh*: None has the right to be worshipped in truth but Allāh"

Sufyān bin Uyaynah– (رَحِمَهُٱللَّه) - said:

مَا أَنْعَمَ اللهُ عَلَى عَبْدٍ مِنَ الْعِبَادِ نِعْمَةً أَعْظَمَ مِنْ أَنْ عَرَّفَهُمْ لَا إِلَهَ إِلَّا اللهُ .

"Allāh has not bestowed a bounty upon his slaves greater than enlightening them with the statement of *Lā Ilaha Illā-Allāh*: None has the right to be worshipped in truth but Allāh"

Amongst its virtues is that Allāh described it in the Qur'ān as the good word, Allāh – (سُبْحَانَهُ وَتَعَالَى) - says:

﴿ أَلَمْ تَرَ كَيْفَ ضَرَبَ ٱللَّهُ مَثَلًا كَلِمَةً طَيِّبَةً كَشَجَرَةٍ طَيِّبَةٍ أَصْلُهَا ثَابِتٌ وَفَرْعُهَا فِي ٱلسَّمَاءِ ۝ تُؤْتِي أُكُلَهَا كُلَّ حِينٍ بِإِذْنِ رَبِّهَا ۗ وَيَضْرِبُ ٱللَّهُ ٱلْأَمْثَالَ لِلنَّاسِ لَعَلَّهُمْ يَتَذَكَّرُونَ ۝ ﴾

"See you not how Allāh sets forth a parable? A goodly word as a goodly tree, whose root is firmly fixed, and its branches (reach) to the sky (i.e. very high). Yielding its fruit at all times, by the permission of its Lord, and Allāh sets forth parables for mankind in order that they may remember." [*Sūrah Ibrāhīm* 14:24-25]

And it is the firm statement referred to in the verse:

$$﴿ يُثَبِّتُ ٱللَّهُ ٱلَّذِينَ ءَامَنُواْ بِٱلْقَوْلِ ٱلثَّابِتِ فِى ٱلْحَيَوٰةِ ٱلدُّنْيَا وَفِى ٱلْأَخِرَةِ وَيُضِلُّ ٱللَّهُ ٱلظَّٰلِمِينَ وَيَفْعَلُ ٱللَّهُ مَا يَشَآءُ ٢٧ ﴾$$

"Allāh will keep firm those who believe, with the word that stands firm in this world (i.e. they will keep on worshipping Allāh Alone and none else), and in the Hereafter. And Allāh will cause to go astray those who are Zālimūn (polytheists and wrong-doers), and Allāh does what He wills." [*Sūrah Ibrāhīm* 14:27]

And it is the promise in the verse:

$$﴿ لَّا يَمْلِكُونَ ٱلشَّفَٰعَةَ إِلَّا مَنِ ٱتَّخَذَ عِندَ ٱلرَّحْمَٰنِ عَهْدًا ٨٧ ﴾$$

"None shall have the power of intercession, but such a one as has received permission (or

promise) from the Most Gracious (Allāh)." [*Sūrah Maryam* 19:87]

It was reported by the way of Ibn Abbas – (رَضِيَ اللَّهُ عَنْهُمَا) - that he said:

الْعَهْدُ : شَهَادَةُ أَنْ لَا إِلَهَ إِلَّا اللهُ ، وَ يَتَبَرَّأُ إِلَى اللهِ عَزَّ

وَ جَلَّ مِنَ الْحَوْلِ وَ الْقُوَّةِ، وَ هِيَ رَأْسُ كُلِّ تَقْوَى .

"The promise is the testimony of *Lā Ilaha Illā-Allāh*: [None has the right to be worshipped in truth but Allāh], and renounce all power and might to Allāh (عَزَّوَجَلَّ), and it (i.e., the statement) is the foremost of any piety."[1]

From amongst its virtues: It is the trustworthy handhold which whoever adheres to it is saved, and whoever abandons it perishes. Allāh (سُبْحَانَهُ وَتَعَالَى) says:

﴿ فَمَن يَكْفُرْ بِالطَّاغُوتِ وَيُؤْمِن بِاللَّهِ فَقَدِ اسْتَمْسَكَ

بِالْعُرْوَةِ الْوُثْقَىٰ ﴾

---

[1] Reported by at-Tabarānī in "*ad-Du'ā*" (3/1518)

"Whoever disbelieves in *Tāghūt* (all false deities) and believes in Allāh, then he has grasped the most trustworthy handhold." [*Sūrah al-Baqarah* 2:256]

And He (سُبْحَانَهُوَتَعَالَى) said:

$$ \text{﴿} * \text{ وَمَن يُسْلِمْ وَجْهَهُۥ إِلَى ٱللَّهِ وَهُوَ مُحْسِنٌ فَقَدِ ٱسْتَمْسَكَ بِٱلْعُرْوَةِ ٱلْوُثْقَىٰ ﴾} $$

"And whosoever submits his face (himself) to Allāh, while he is a Muhsin (good-doer i.e. performs good deeds totally for Allāh's sake without any show off or to gain praise or fame and does them in accordance with the Sunnah of Allāh's Messenger Muhammad (صَلَّىٰاللَّهُعَلَيْهِوَسَلَّمَ)), then he has grasped the most trustworthy handhold [*Lā Ilaha Illā-Allāh* (none has the right to be worshipped but Allāh)]." [*Sūrah Luqmān* 31:22]

Among its virtues: It is the lasting word that Ibrāhīm (عَلَيْهِالسَّلَام) has left behind in his posterity. Allāh (سُبْحَانَهُوَتَعَالَى) says:

VIRTUES OF THE STATEMENT: "NONE HAS THE RIGHT TO BE WORSHIPPED IN TRUTH BUT ALLĀH."

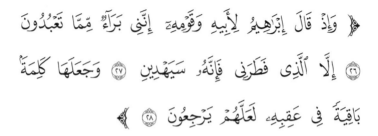

﴿ وَإِذْ قَالَ إِبْرَٰهِيمُ لِأَبِيهِ وَقَوْمِهِ إِنَّنِي بَرَآءٌ مِّمَّا تَعْبُدُونَ ۝ إِلَّا ٱلَّذِى فَطَرَنِي فَإِنَّهُۥ سَيَهْدِينِ ۝ وَجَعَلَهَا كَلِمَةَۢ بَاقِيَةً فِى عَقِبِهِۦ لَعَلَّهُمْ يَرْجِعُونَ ۝ ﴾

"And (remember) when Ibrāhīm (Abraham) said to his father and his people: "Verily, I am innocent of what you worship, 'Except Him (i.e. I worship none but Allāh Alone) Who did create me; and verily He will guide me.' And he made it [i.e. *Lā Ilaha Illā-Allāh* (none has the right to be worshipped in truth but Allāh Alone)] a Word lasting among his offspring, (True Monotheism), that they may turn back (i.e. to repent to Allāh or receive admonition)." [*Sūrah az-Zukhruf* 43:26-28]

It is the word of piety that Allāh made the companions of the Messenger (ﷺ) hold to and made them worthy of it, Allāh (سُبْحَانَهُ وَتَعَالَى) says:

﴿ إِذْ جَعَلَ ٱلَّذِينَ كَفَرُوا۟ فِى قُلُوبِهِمُ ٱلْحَمِيَّةَ حَمِيَّةَ ٱلْجَٰهِلِيَّةِ فَأَنزَلَ ٱللَّهُ سَكِينَتَهُۥ عَلَىٰ رَسُولِهِۦ وَعَلَى

ٱلۡمُؤۡمِنِينَ وَأَلۡزَمَهُمۡ كَلِمَةَ ٱلتَّقۡوَىٰ وَكَانُوٓاْ أَحَقَّ بِهَا وَأَهۡلَهَاۚ وَكَانَ ٱللَّهُ بِكُلِّ شَىۡءٍ عَلِيمًا ٢٦

"When those who disbelieve had put in their hearts pride and haughtiness - the pride and haughtiness of the time of ignorance, - then Allāh sent down His *Sakīnah* (calmness and tranquility) upon His Messenger (صَلَّىٱللَّهُعَلَيۡهِوَسَلَّمَ) and upon the believers, and made them stick to the word of piety (i.e. none has the right to be worshipped in truth but Allāh); and they were well entitled to it and worthy of it. And Allāh is the All-Knower of everything." [*Sūrah al-Fath* 48:26]

Abū Ishāq as-Sabi'ye narrated from Amr bin Maymūn that he said:

مَا تَكَلَّمَ النَّاسُ بِشَيۡءٍ أَفۡضَلَ مِنۡ لَا إِلَهَ إِلَّا اللهُ

"Mankind has not made mention of a word better than *Lā Ilaha Illā-Allāh* (none has the right to be worshipped in truth but Allāh Alone)."

So Sa'ad bin 'Iyādh said in reply:

VIRTUES OF THE STATEMENT: "NONE HAS THE RIGHT TO BE WORSHIPPED IN TRUTH BUT ALLĀH."

أَ تَدْرِي مَا هِيَ يَا أَبَا عَبْدِ الله ؟ هِيَ وَ اللهِ كَلِمَةُ

التَّقْوَى أَلْزَمَهَا اللهُ أَصْحَابَ مُحَمَّدٍ صَلَّى اللهُ عَلَيْهِ

وَ سَلَّمَ وَ كَانُوا أَحَقَّ بِهَا وَ أَهْلَهَا رَضِيَ اللهُ عَنْهُمْ

"Do you know what that word actually is? By Allāh it is the word of piety that Allāh made the companions of Prophet Muhammad (ﷺ) adhere to and made them worthy of it – (رَضِيَاللَّهَُعَنْهُمْ)."[2]

Also among its virtues: It is the utmost propriety. Allāh (سُبْحَانَهُوَتَعَالَى) says:

﴿ يَوْمَ يَقُومُ ٱلرُّوحُ وَٱلْمَلَٰئِكَةُ صَفًّا لَّا يَتَكَلَّمُونَ إِلَّا مَنْ أَذِنَ لَهُ ٱلرَّحْمَٰنُ وَقَالَ صَوَابًا ۝ ﴾

"The Day that Ar-Rūh [Jibrīl (Gabriel) or another angel] and the angels will stand forth in rows, they will not speak except him whom the Most Gracious (Allāh) allows, and he will speak what is right." [Sūrah an-Naba' 78:38]

---

[2] Reported by at-Tabarānī in *ad-Du'ā* (3/15133)

'Alī bin Abī Talha reported from ibn 'Abbas (رَضِيَٱللَّهُعَنْهُمَا) regarding: (**speak except him whom the Most Gracious (Allāh) allows, and he will speak what is right.**) that he said its meaning to be:

$$ إِلَّا مَنْ أَذِنَ لَـهُ الـرَّبُّ عَـزَّ وَ جَـلَّ بِـشَـهَـادَةِ أَنْ لَا إِلَـهَ إِلَّا اللهُ ، وَ هِيَ مُنْتَـهَى الـصَّـوَابِ . $$

"Except whom the Lord (عَزَّوَجَلَّ) allows by the testimony of *Lā Ilaha Illā-Allāh* (none has the right to be worshipped in truth but Allāh Alone), and it is the ultimate rightness." [3]

Also Ikrimah – (رَحِمَهُٱللَّهُ) –said:

$$ الـصَّـوَابُ : لَا إِلَـهَ إِلَّا اللهُ $$

"The rightness is: *Lā Ilaha Illā-Allāh* (none has the right to be worshipped in truth but Allāh Alone)." [4]

Also among its virtues is that it's the true calling mentioned in the saying of Allāh (سُبْحَانَهُوَتَعَالَى):

---

[3] At-Tabarānī reported it in the book "*Du'ā*" (3/1533)
[4] At-Tabarānī reported it in the book "*Du'ā*" (3/1520)

VIRTUES OF THE STATEMENT: "NONE HAS THE RIGHT TO BE WORSHIPPED IN TRUTH BUT ALLĀH."

"For Him (Allāh, Alone) is the Word of Truth (i.e. none has the right to be worshipped but Allāh). And those whom they (polytheists and disbelievers) invoke, answer them no more than one who stretches forth his hand (at the edge of a deep well) for water to reach his mouth, but it reaches him not; and the invocation of the disbelievers is nothing but an error (i.e. of no use)." [*Sūrah ar-Rūm* 13:14]

Furthermore, it is the real bond that unites the followers of the Islāmic religion. By this statement the lines of love, allegiance, and enmity are drawn. As a result, the Islāmic society has become firmly connected as one body, each part strengthening and supporting another.

The Scholar, Shaikh Muhammad al-Amīn Shinqītī stated in his book *Adwaa' al-Bayān:*

> **"In conclusion, the true bond that brings together the discordant is the bond of *Lā Ilaha***

Illā-Allāh (none has the right to be worshipped in truth but Allāh Alone). It is apparent that this bond has warmed the hearts of those who bear the throne of the angels for mankind on earth, despite their differences. Allāh (سُبْحَانَهُوَتَعَالَى) said:

﴿ ٱلَّذِينَ يَحْمِلُونَ ٱلْعَرْشَ وَمَنْ حَوْلَهُۥ يُسَبِّحُونَ بِحَمْدِ رَبِّهِمْ وَيُؤْمِنُونَ بِهِۦ وَيَسْتَغْفِرُونَ لِلَّذِينَ ءَامَنُواْ رَبَّنَا وَسِعْتَ كُلَّ شَىْءٍ رَّحْمَةً وَعِلْمًا فَٱغْفِرْ لِلَّذِينَ تَابُواْ وَٱتَّبَعُواْ سَبِيلَكَ وَقِهِمْ عَذَابَ ٱلْجَحِيمِ ۝ رَبَّنَا وَأَدْخِلْهُمْ جَنَّٰتِ عَدْنٍ ٱلَّتِى وَعَدتَّهُمْ وَمَن صَلَحَ مِنْ ءَابَآئِهِمْ وَأَزْوَٰجِهِمْ وَذُرِّيَّٰتِهِمْ إِنَّكَ أَنتَ ٱلْعَزِيزُ ٱلْحَكِيمُ ۝ وَقِهِمُ ٱلسَّيِّـَٔاتِ وَمَن تَقِ ٱلسَّيِّـَٔاتِ يَوْمَئِذٍ فَقَدْ رَحِمْتَهُۥ وَذَٰلِكَ هُوَ ٱلْفَوْزُ ٱلْعَظِيمُ ۝ ﴾

"Those (angels) who bear the Throne (of Allāh) and those around it glorify the praises of their Lord, and believe in Him, and ask forgiveness for those who believe (in the Oneness of Allāh) (saying): "Our Lord! You comprehend all things in mercy and knowledge, so forgive those who repent and follow Your Way, and save them from the torment of the blazing Fire! "Our Lord! And make them enter the 'Adn (Eden) Paradise (everlasting Gardens) which you have promised them - and to the righteous among their fathers, their wives, and their offspring! Verily, You are the All-Mighty, the All-Wise. "And save them from (the punishment, for what they did of) the sins, and whomsoever You save from (the punishment for what he did of) the sins (i.e. pardon him) that Day, him verily, You have taken into mercy." And that is the supreme success." [*Sūrah Ghāfir* 40:7-9]

The verses indicate that the bond that gripped the angels bearing the throne to mankind on Earth, compelling them to seek from Allāh such magnificent prayer for humanity, could only be the belief in Allāh (جَلَّوَعَلَا)."

Continuing on, he said- (رَحِمَهُ أَللَّهُ):

"Overall, there is no dispute amongst Muslims that the bond that unites the dwellers of the earth and the dwellers of the heavens is the bond of *Lā Ilaha Illā-Allāh* (none has the right to be worshipped in truth but Allāh Alone). So, it is not permissible to call to any other bond."[5]

<u>And amongst the virtues</u>: It is the best of good deeds. Allāh (سُبْحَانَهُوَتَعَالَی) says:

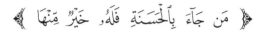

"Whoever brings a good deed will have better than its worth." [*Sūrah an-Nahl* 16:89]

Ibn Mas'ūd, Ibn Abbas, Abu Huraira, and others have reported in regards to the good deed mentioned: It is *Lā Ilaha Illā-Allāh* (none has the right to be worshipped in truth but Allāh Alone)[6]

Also reported from Ikrimah- (رَحِمَهُٱللَّهُ) - regarding the statement of Allāh (عَزَّوَجَلَّ):

"Whoever brings a good deed will have better than its worth" that he said: "It is *Lā Ilaha Illā-Allāh* (none has the right to be worshipped in truth but Allāh Alone), and the intended meaning is that: *he will the attain the good from it*. Reason being that there is nothing better than

---

[5] *Adwa' al-Bayān* (3/447-448)
[6] Ad-Du'ā by At-Tabarānī (3/1497-1498)

VIRTUES OF THE STATEMENT: "NONE HAS THE RIGHT TO BE WORSHIPPED IN TRUTH BUT ALLĀH."

Lā Ilaha Illā-Allāh **(none has the right to be worshipped in truth but Allāh Alone"[7]**

It has been affirmed in *al-Musnad* by the way of Abū Dhar (رَضِيَاللهُعَنْهُ) that he said:

يَا رَسُولَ اللهِ ، عَلِّمْنِي عَمَلاً يُقَرِّبُنِي مِنَ الْجَنَّةِ وَ يُبَاعِدُنِي مِنَ النَّارِ .

"Tell me what will bring me near to the Garden and keep me far from the Fire."

He (صَلَّىاللهُعَلَيْهِوَسَلَّمَ) said:

إِذَا عَمِلْتَ سَيِّئَةً فَاعْمَلْ حَسَنَةً فَإِنَّهَا عَشْرُ أَمْثَالِهَا .

"If you commit an evil deed then do a good deed; it is in ten folds,"

I said,

يَا رَسُولَ اللهِ ، أَ فَمِنَ الْحَسَنَاتِ لَا إِلَهَ إِلَّا اللهُ ؟

---

[7] *"Fadhl At-Tahlīl wa Thawābuh Al-Jazīl"* by Ibn al-Banna; p.74

"O' Messenger of Allāh, is among the good deeds *Lā Ilaha Illā-Allāh?"*

He (صَلَّى ٱللَّهُ عَلَيْهِ وَسَلَّمَ) replied,

نَعَمْ ، هِيَ أَحْسَنُ الْحَسَنَاتِ

"Yes, it is the best of good deeds."[8]

---

8 Al-Musnad; (5/169), and *ad-Du'ā* by at-Tabarānī; No. 1489

MORE VIRTUES OF THIS STATEMENT AS RECORDED IN THE SUNNAH

We have previously discussed the virtues of *Lā Ilaha Illā-Allāh* as established in the Qur'an al-Karim, affirming that it is the reason for creating the heavens and earth and all that exists. For its call the Messengers were sent, books were revealed, and legislations established. For its cause, scales of the Hereafter were placed, deeds recorded, Paradise and Fire created, and people divided into believers and disbelievers.

Therefore, it is the truth which the entire religion is founded upon, and to it will be held accountable those of the past later times. Evidently, on the Day of Judgment a servant will not proceed until he is questioned about two things: What have you worshipped, and what was your reply to the Messengers? The answer to the first is the actualization of the word of *Tawhīd* (i.e. monotheism: *Lā Ilaha Illā-Allāh* - none has the right to be worshipped in truth but Allāh Alone), while the answer to the second is the actualization of the testimony that Muhammad (صَلَّى ٱللَّهُ عَلَيْهِ وَسَلَّمَ) is the Messenger of Allāh; in acknowledgment, admission, and obedience.

Indeed, the virtues of the word of *Tawhīd* are abundant, surpassing beyond what one could enumerate. Here will be an attempt to present some of its virtues as recorded in the *hadith* (verbal traditions) of the Prophet (ﷺ).

Among its virtues: It is the most virtuous of deeds, the reward of which is equivalent to freeing a slave, and it is a protection from *Shaytān*. It has been reported from the way of Abu Hurayrah (رضي الله عنه) that the Messenger (ﷺ) said:

مَنْ قَالَ: لَا إِلَهَ إِلَّا اللهُ وَحْدَهُ لَا شَرِيكَ لَهُ، لَهُ الْمُلْكُ وَ لَهُ الْحَمْدُ وَ هُوَ عَلَى كُلِّ شَيْءٍ قَدِيرٌ فِي يَوْمٍ مِائَةَ مَرَّةٍ كَانَتْ لَهُ عَدْلُ عَشْرِ رِقَابٍ، وَ كُتِبَتْ لَهُ مِائَةُ حَسَنَةٍ، وَ مُحِيَتْ عَنْهُ مِائَةُ سَيِّئَةٍ، وَ كَانَتْ لَهُ حِرْزًا مِنَ الشَّيْطَانِ يَوْمَهُ ذَلِكَ حَتَّى يُمْسِيَ، وَ لَمْ يَأْتِ أَحَدٌ بِأَفْضَلَ مِمَّا جَاءَ بِهِ، إِلَّا أَحَدٌ عَمِلَ أَكْثَرَ مِنْ ذَلِكَ.

"Whoever says There is no god but Allāh, alone, without any partner, the Kingdom and praise belong to Him and He has power over everything' (*Lā Ilaha Illā-Allāh, wahdahu la sharīka lahu, lahul-mulku wa lahul-hamdu, wa huwa ala kulli shay'in qadīr*) one hundred times a day, it is the same for him as freeing ten slaves. One hundred good actions are written for him and one hundred wrong actions are erased from him, and it is a protection from Shaytan for that day until the night. No-one does anything more excellent than what he does except someone who does more than that." [Al-Bukhari and Muslim].[9]

Also Abū Ayyub al-Ansārī (رَضِىَاللَّهُعَنْهُ) reported: The Prophet (صَلَّىاللَّهُعَلَيْهِوَسَلَّمَ) said:

مَنْ قَالَهَا عَشْرَ مَرَّاتٍ كَانَ كَمَنْ أَعْتَقَ أَرْبَعَةَ أَنْفُسٍ مِنْ وَلَدِ إِسْمَاعِيلَ .

"He who utters ten times: '*Lā Ilaha Illā-Allāh, wahdahu lā sharīka lahu, lahul-mulku wa lahul-hamdu, wa Huwa 'alā kulli shay'in Qadīr* (there is no true god except Allāh. He is One and He has no partner with Him. His is the sovereignty and His is the praise, and He is Omnipotent),' he will have a reward equal to that for freeing four slaves

---

[9] Al-Bukhārī: No.6403, Muslim; No. 2691

from the progeny of Prophet Ismā'il." [Al-
Bukhari and Muslim].[10]

<u>From among its virtues:</u> It is the best statement uttered
by the Messengers as reported from the Prophet
(صَلَّىاللَّهُعَلَيْهِوَسَلَّمَ) that he said:

أَفْضَلُ مَا قُلْتُ أَنَا وَ النَّبِيُّوْنَ عَشِيَّةَ عَرَفَةَ : لَا إِلَهَ

إِلَّا اللهُ وَحْدَهُ لَا شَرِيكَ لَهُ ، لَهُ الْمُلْكُ وَ لَهُ الْحَمْدُ

وَ هُوَ عَلَى كُلِّ شَيْءٍ قَدِيرٌ .

"**The most virtuous of what I and the Prophets
said in the afternoon of 'Arafah is: None has the
right to be worshipped but Allāh, alone, without
partner, to Him belongs all that exists, and to
Him belongs the Praise, and He is powerful over
all things. (La Ilaha Illā-Allāh, wahdahu lā
sharīka lahu, lahul-mulku wa lahul-hamdu, wa
huwa `alā kulli shay'in qadīr)."** [11]

In similar wording,

---

[10] Al-Bukhārī: No.6404, Muslim; No. 2693
[11] At-Tabarānī in "ad-Du'ā'"; No.874

خَيْرُ الدُّعَاءِ دُعَاءُ يَوْمِ عَرَفَةَ، وَ خَيْرُ مَا قُلْتُهُ أَنَا وَ

النَّبِيُّونَ مِنْ قَبْلِي : لَا إِلَهَ إِلَّا اللهُ وَحْدَهُ لَا شَرِيكَ لَهُ

، لَهُ الْمُلْكُ وَ لَهُ الْحَمْدُ وَ هُوَ عَلَى كُلِّ شَيْءٍ قَدِيرٌ

"The best of supplication is the supplication of
the Day of `Arafah. And the best of what I and
the Prophets before me have said is: None has the
right to be worshipped but Allāh, alone, without
partner, to Him belongs all that exists, and to
Him belongs the Praise, and He is powerful over
all things. (*Lā Ilaha Illā-Allāh, wahdahu lā
sharīka lahu, lahul-mulku wa lahul-hamdu, wa
huwa `alā kulli shai'in qadīr*)." [12]

From its virtues: It sways the scrolls of mischief and sinful
deeds on the Day of Judgment, as is stated in the *hadith* of
'Abdullah bin 'Amr bin al-'As (رَضِيَٱللَّهُعَنْهُ), that the Prophet
(صَلَّىٱللَّهُعَلَيْهِوَسَلَّمَ) said:

يُصَاحُ بِرَجُلٍ مِنْ أُمَّتِي عَلَى رُؤُوسِ الْخَلَائِقِ يَوْمَ

الْقِيَامَةِ، فَيُنْشَرُ لَهُ تِسْعَةٌ وَ تِسْعُونَ سِجِلًّا، كُلُّ

سِجِلٍّ مِنْهَا مَدَّ الْبَصَرِ ، ثُمَّ يَقُولُ اللهُ تَبَارَكَ وَ

---

[12] Jami` at-Tirmidhi; No. 3585

تَعَالَى لَهُ : أَ تُنْكِرُ مِنْ هَذَا شَيْئًا؟ فَيَقُولُ : لَا يَا رَبِّ . فَيَقُولُ عَزَّ وَ جَلَّ : أَ لَكَ عُذْرٌ أَوْ حَسَنَةٌ؟ فَيَهَابُ الرَّجُلُ فَيَقُولُ : لَا يَا رَبِّ . فَيَقُولُ عَزَّ وَ جَلَّ : بَلَى إِنَّ لَكَ عِنْدَنَا حَسَنَةً ، وَ إِنَّهُ لَا ظُلْمَ عَلَيْكَ ، فَتُخْرَجُ لَهُ بِطَاقَةٌ فِيهَا : أَشْهَدُ أَنْ لَا إِلَهَ إِلَّا اللهُ وَ أَنَّ مُحَمَّدًا عَبْدُهُ وَ رَسُولُهُ ، فَيَقُولُ : يَا رَبِّ مَا هَذِهِ الْبِطَاقَةُ مَعَ هَذِهِ السِّجِلَّاتِ ؟! فَيَقُولُ عَزَّ وَ جَلَّ : إِنَّكَ لَا تُظْلَمُ ، قَالَ : فَتُوضَعُ السِّجِلَّاتُ فِي كِفَّةٍ وَالْبِطَاقَةُ فِي كِفَّةٍ ، فَطَاشَتِ السِّجِلَّاتُ وَ ثَقُلَتِ الْبِطَاقَةُ .

"A man from my nation will be called before all of creation on the Day of Resurrection, and ninety-nine scrolls will be spread out for him, each one extending as far as the eye can see. Then Allāh will say: "Do you deny anything of this?" He will say: "No, O Lord." He will say: "Have My recording scribes been unfair to you?" Then He will say: "Apart from that, do you have any good deeds?" The man will be terrified and will say:

"No." (Allāh) will say: "Indeed, you have good deeds with Us, and you will not be treated unjustly this Day." Then a card will be brought out on which is written *Ash-hadu an Lā Ilaha Illā-Allāh wa anna Muhammadan 'abduhu wa rasūluhu* (I bear witness that none has the right to be worshipped but Allāh, and that Muhammad is His slave and Messenger). He will say: "O Lord, what is this card compared with these scrolls?" He will say: "You will not be treated unjustly." Then the scrolls will be placed in one side of the Balance and the card in the other. The scrolls will go up (i.e., be light) and the card will go down (i.e., will weigh heavily)."[13]

Certainly, there is a significant presence of *Īmān* (faith) in his heart to have the card of *Lā Ilaha Illā-Allāh* sway those scrolls. The people vary in deeds (i.e. in its reward and acceptance) based on the strength of *Īmān* in their heart. Hence, the reason for those that utter the same statement: *Lā Ilaha Illā-Allāh*, but do not attain the same reward is due to a weakness of *Īmān* in the heart. This is evident from the *hadith* of Anas bin Mālik (رَضِىَٱللَّهُعَنْهُ) that the Prophet (صَلَّىٱللَّهُعَلَيْهِوَسَلَّمَ) said:

---

[13] *Al-Musnad* (2/213). Jami` at-Tirmidhī; No. 2639. *Sunan* ibn Mājah; No. 4300. Rated authentic by al-Albānī in "Saḥīḥ Al-Jami'"; No. 8095

يَخْرُجُ مِنَ النَّارِ مَنْ قَالَ : لَا إِلَهَ إِلَّا اللهُ وَ فِي قَلْبِهِ
وَزْنُ شَعِيرَةٍ مِنْ خَيْرٍ ، وَ يَخْرُجُ مِنَ النَّارِ مَنْ قَالَ
لَا إِلَهَ إِلَّا اللهُ وَ فِي قَلْبِهِ وَزْنُ بُرَّةٍ مِنْ خَيْرٍ ، وَ يَخْرُجُ
مِنَ النَّارِ مَنْ قَالَ لَا إِلَهَ إِلَّا اللهُ وَ فِي قَلْبِهِ وَزْنُ ذَرَّةٍ
مِنْ خَيْرٍ .

"Whoever said, "None has the right to be worshipped but Allāh and has in his heart good (faith) equal to the weight of a barley grain will be taken out of Hell. And whoever said: "None has the right to be worshipped but Allāh and has in his heart good (faith) equal to the weight of a wheat grain will be taken out of Hell. And whoever said, "None has the right to be worshipped but Allāh and has in his heart good (faith) equal to the weight of an atom will be taken out of Hell." [14]

Therefore, the people of *Lā Ilaha Illā-Allāh* vary in their rewards based on the goodness of *Īmān* in their hearts.

---

[14] Al-Bukhārī; No. 44. Muslim; No. 193, 325

Among the virtues of this word: It overweighs the heavens and earth as indicated in the *hadith* of Abdullah bin 'Amr (رَضِيَٱللَّهُعَنْهُ), the Prophet (صَلَّىٱللَّهُعَلَيْهِوَسَلَّمَ) said:

أَنَّ نُوحاً قَالَ لِابْنِهِ عِنْدَ مَوْتِهِ : آمُرُكَ بِـلَا إِلَـهَ إِلَّا اللهُ ، فَإِنَّ السَّمَاوَتِ السَّبْعَ وَ الْأَرَضِـينَ السَّبْعَ لَوْ وُضِعَتْ فِي كِفَّةٍ ، وَ وُضِعَتْ : لَا إِلَهَ إِلَّا اللهُ فِي كِفَّةٍ رَجَحَتْ بِهِنَّ لَا إِلَهَ إِلَّا اللهُ ، وَ لَوْ أَنَّ السَّمَـواتِ السَّبْعَ كُنَّ حَلَقَةً مُبْهَمَةً لَقَصَمَتْهُنَّ لَا إِلَهَ إِلَّا اللهُ.

"Noah, at his death bed, had said to his son ' I command you to hold to *Lā Ilaha Illā-Allāh*, for it the seven heavens and the seven earths are placed on one side of the scale's balance while *Lā Ilaha Illā-Allāh* is placed on the other side. Surely *Lā Ilaha Illā-Allāh* would sway them. And if the seven heavens were to be an enclosed ring, then *Lā Ilaha Illā-Allāh* would shatter it." [15]

---

[15] Al-Musnad; 2/170. Rated as authentic by al-Albānī in "*Silsilah As-Saḥīahi*"; No. 134

Among its virtues: There is no barrier to veil it from Allāh. Rather, it penetrates all barriers, as reported in the *hadith* of Abu Hurayrah (رَضِيَاللَّهُعَنْهُ), that the Prophet (صَلَّىاللَّهُعَلَيْهِوَسَلَّمَ) said:

مَا قَالَ عَبْدٌ: لَا إِلَهَ إِلَّا اللهُ قَطُّ مُخْلِصاً، إِلَّا فُتِحَتْ لَهُ أَبْوَابُ السَّمَاءِ حَتَّى تُفْضِيَ إِلَى الْعَرْشِ، مَا اجْتَنَبَ الْكَبَائِرَ.

"No worshipper has ever said: None has the right to be worshipped but Allāh (*Lā Ilaha Illā-Allāh*)' sincerely, except that the gates of heaven are opened for it, until it reaches to the Throne, so long as he avoids the major sins."[16]

From its virtues: It is a salvation from the Fire according to a narration that the Prophet (صَلَّىاللَّهُعَلَيْهِوَسَلَّمَ) heard a man making *Adhān* (call to prayer), saying *Ash-hadu an Lā Ilaha Illā-Allāh* (I bear witness none has the right to be worshipped in truth but Allāh). He (صَلَّىاللَّهُعَلَيْهِوَسَلَّمَ) said:

خَرَجَ مِنَ النَّارِ

---

[16] Jami` at-Tirmidhī; No. 3590. Of a sound narration Rated as *Hasan* by al-Albānī

"He is saved from the Fire"[17]

Also in the *hadith* of 'Itbān (رَضِوَٱللَّهُعَنهُ) that the Prophet
(صَلَّىٱللَّهُعَلَيهِوَسَلَّمَ) said:

إِنَّ اللهَ حَرَّمَ عَـلَـى الـنَّـارِ مَـنْ قَـالَ : لَا إِلَـهَ إِلَّا اللهُ ، يَـبْـتَـغِـي

بِـذَلِـكَ وَجْـهَ اللهِ .

**"Allāh has made the fire of Hell unlawful for him
who affirms that none has the right to be
worshipped but Allāh."[18]**

<u>**From the virtues of this statement:**</u> Is that the Prophet
(صَلَّىٱللَّهُعَلَيهِوَسَلَّمَ) made it the most virtuous branch of Īmān. In
the two Sahīh from the *hadīth* of Abū Hurayrah (رَضِيَ) the
Prophet (صَلَّىٱللَّهُعَلَيهِوَسَلَّمَ) said,

الْإِيـمَـانُ بِـضْـعٌ وَ سَـبْـعُـونَ شُـعْـبَـةً، أَعْـلَاهَا قَـوْلُ لَا إِلَـهَ

إِلَّا اللهُ ، وَ أَدْنَـاهَـا إِمَـاطَـةُ الْأَذَى عَـنِ الـطَّـرِيـقِ .

**"Īmān is made up of seventy odd number of
branches. The highest is the statement 'none has
the right to be worshipped in truth but Allaah'**

---

[17] Muslim; No. 382
[18] Al-Bukhārī; No. 6938. Muslim; No. 33, 263

and the lowest branch is to remove harm out of the road." [19]

From its virtues: It is the most virtuous supplication, as in the *hadith* of Jābir bin Abdullāh (رَضِيَاللَّهُعَنْهُ), when he said, "I heard the Prophet (صَلَّىاللَّهُعَلَيْهِوَسَلَّمَ) say:

أَفْضَلُ الـذِّكْرِ : لَا إِلَهَ إِلَّا اللهُ ، وَ أَفْضَلُ الـدُّعَاءِ :
الْحَمْدُ لله .

"The best of remembrance is *Lā Ilaha Illā-Allāh* (None has the right to be worshipped in truth but Allāh), and the best of supplication is *al-Hamdu Lillāhi* (praise is to Allāh)." [20]

Amongst its virtues: Whoever says it sincerely from his heart will be most fortunate; included in the intercession of the Prophet (صَلَّىاللَّهُعَلَيْهِوَسَلَّمَ) on the Day of Judgment, as in the *hadith* of Abu Hurayrah (رَضِيَاللَّهُعَنْهُ):

يَا رَسُولَ اللهِ ، مَنْ أَسْعَدَ النَّاسِ بِشِفَاعَتِكَ يَوْمَ
الْقِيَامَةِ ؟ قَالَ رَسُولُ اللهِ صَلَّى اللهُ عَلَيْهِ وَ سَلَّمَ : ((

---

[19] Al-Bukhārī; No. 9. Muslim; No. 35.
[20] Jami` at-Tirmidhī; No. 3383. Sunan Ibn Mājah; No. 3800. Rated *Hassan* by al-Albānī in *Sahīh al-Jami'*; No.1104

لَقَدْ ظَنَنْتُ يَا أَبَا هُرَيْرَةَ أَنْ لَا يَسْأَلَنِي عَنْ هَذَا

الْحَدِيثِ أَحَدٌ أَوَّلَ مِنْكَ ، لِمَا رَأَيْتُ مِنْ حِرْصِكَ

عَلَى الْحَدِيثِ ، أَسْعَدُ النَّاسِ بِشِفَاعَتِي يَوْمَ

الْقِيَامَةِ : مَنْ قَالَ : لَا إِلَهَ إِلَّا اللهُ ، خَالِصاً مِنْ قَلْبِهِ

أَوْ نَفْسِهِ)) .

"I said: O Allāh's Messenger (صَلَّىاللَّهُعَلَيْهِوَسَلَّمَ)! Who
will be the luckiest person who will gain your
intercession on the Day of Resurrection?" Allāh's
Messenger (صَلَّىاللَّهُعَلَيْهِوَسَلَّمَ) said: "O Abu Hurayrah! I
have thought that none will ask me about this
before you, as I know your longing for the
(learning of) *hadīth*. The luckiest person who
will have my intercession on the Day of
Resurrection will be the one who said sincerely
from the bottom of his heart 'none has the right
to be worshipped in truth but Allāh.'"[21]

It is evident from the past *Hadīth* in particular the
statement: "**the one who said sincerely from the
bottom of his heart 'None has the right to be
worshipped in truth but Allāh,**" that the invocation of

---

[21] *Sahīh al-Bukhārī*; No. 99.

this word is not accepted by mere utterance upon the tongue. Rather, one must abide by its conditions mentioned in the Qur'ān and Sunnah.

CONDITIONS OF *LĀ ILAHA ILLĀ-ALLĀH*

We have previously mentioned the virtues of the word of *Tawhīd* (monotheism): *Lā Ilaha Illā-Allāh*. We have confirmed that it is the best of statements and most virtuous of all, and presented the resulting noble reward and beneficial fruits of it in this life and the hereafter.

However, every Muslim must know that *Lā Ilaha Illā-Allāh* is not accepted by merely uttering it on the tongue. Rather, it is a must to fulfill its due rights, and establish its conditions as outlined in the Qur'ān and the *Sunnah* (صَلَّاللَّهُعَلَيْهِوَسَلَّمَ). Every Muslim is aware that no act of obedience to Allāh is accepted unless its conditions are fulfilled. For example, the *Salah* (prayer) is not accepted without its established conditions, *Hajj* (pilgrimage) is not accepted without its conditions, and likewise any other act of worship is not accepted without its defined conditions in the Qur'ān and *Sunnah*. Similarly, the invocation of the Statement: *Lā Ilaha Illā-Allāh*, will not be accepted from an individual without its conditions detailed in the Qur'ān and *Sunnah*.

The righteous predecessors have indicated the importance of giving due diligence to the conditions of *Lā Ilaha Illā-Allāh* and the obligation of adhering to it. As such, it was reported from *Hassan Al – Basri* that it was said to him: "Some people are saying: 'Whoever says *Lā Ilaha Illā-Allāh* enters Paradise"!

He said: "Whoever says *Lā Ilaha Illā-Allāh* and accomplish its rights and obligations, will enter Jannah"

In addition, in other reports *Hassan Al-Basri* said to *Farazdaq,* as he was burying his deceased wife:

مَا أَعْدَدتَّ لِهَذَا الْيَوْم ؟ قَالَ : شَهَادَةُ أَنْ لَا إِلَهَ إِلَّا اللهُ مُنْذُ سَبْعِينَ سَنَةً . فَقَالَ الْحَسَنُ : نِعْمَ الْعُدَّة ، لَكِنْ لِلَا إِلَهَ إِلَّا اللهُ شُرُوطٌ ، فَإِيَّاكَ وَ قَذْفَ الْمُحْصَنَاتِ .

"What have you prepared for such day (i.e., death)?"

He (*Farazdaq*) said: "A testimony of *Lā Ilaha Illā-Allāh* of seventy years."

Hassan replied: "Indeed, it is the best apparatus, but there are conditions for *Lā Ilaha Illā-Allāh.* So, abstain from accusing innocent women of adultery."

Ibn Munabih was once asked:

أَ لَيْسَ مِفْتَاحُ الْجَنَّةِ لَا إِلَهَ إِلَّا اللهُ؟ قَالَ: بَلَى، وَ
لَكِنْ مَا مِنْ مِفْتَاحٍ إِلَّا لَهُ أَسْنَانٌ، فَإِنْ أَتَيْتَ
بِمِفْتَاحٍ لَهُ أَسْنَانٌ فُتِحَ لَكَ، وَ إِلَّا لَمْ يُفْتَحْ،))
يُشِيرُ بِالْأَسْنَانِ إِلَى شُرُوطِ: لَا إِلَهَ إِلَّا اللهُ)).

"Isn't the statement of *Lā Ilaha Illā-Allāh* the key to the Paradise?"

He answered, "Yes, but every key has ridges. If you come with the key that has the right ridges, the door will open for you. If you do not have the right ridges the door will not open for you."[22]

The ridges mentioned are referring to the conditions of *Lā Ilaha Illā-Allāh*.

An in-depth study of the texts of the Qur'ān and *Sunnah* reveal that the statement of *Lā Ilaha Illā-Allāh* will not be accepted without the following seven conditions:

1. Knowledge of its meaning, which negates ignorance.
2. Certainty which negates doubt.
3. Sincerity which negates polytheism and hypocrisy.

---

[22] These reports are recorded by *Ibn Rajab* in **Kalimatul Ikhlās** p. 14

4. Truthfulness as opposed to dishonesty.
5. Love which negates hate and abomination.
6. Submission and Compliance as opposed to neglect.
7. Acceptance that negates rejection.

Some of the people of knowledge placed these seven conditions in a line poetry, saying:

$$\text{عِلْمٌ يَقِينٌ وَ إِخْلَاصٌ وَ صِدْقُكَ مَعْ}$$

$$\text{مَحَبَّةٍ وَانْقِيَادٍ وَ الْقَبُولُ لَهَا}$$

"Knowledge, Certainty, Sincerity, and your truthfulness along with love, yielding and acceptance of these conditions."

We shall look further into each condition to discover its significance while referencing some of its proofs from the Qur'ān and *Sunnah*.[23]

The first Condition: Knowledge (*al-'Ilm*) of the meaning of this statement that negates ignorance. Thus, it is vital to know that it negates all forms of worship from anyone

---

[23] For detailed commentary refer to: *Ma'arij Al-Qabul* by Shaykh Hafidh al-Hakami p. 1/377 and on.

other than Allāh, and it affirms all of it to Allāh alone. As Allāh (سُبْحَانَهُوَتَعَالَى) says:

﴿ إِيَّاكَ نَعْبُدُ وَإِيَّاكَ نَسْتَعِينُ ۝ ﴾

"You (Alone) we worship, and You (Alone) we ask for help (for each and everything). " [*Sūrah al-Fatihah* 1:5]

Meaning: We worship You alone and worship none other, and we seek help from You alone and seek it from none other than You.

Allāh (سُبْحَانَهُوَتَعَالَى) said:

﴿ فَٱعْلَمْ أَنَّهُ لَا إِلَهَ إِلَّا ٱللَّهُ ﴾

"So know (O Muhammad (صَلَّىٱللَّهُعَلَيْهِوَسَلَّمَ)) that, *Lā Ilaha Illā-Allāh* (none has the right to be worshipped in truth but Allāh)." [*Sūrah Muhammad* 47:19]

Moreover, He (سُبْحَانَهُوَتَعَالَى) also said:

﴿ إِلَّا مَن شَهِدَ بِٱلْحَقِّ وَهُمْ يَعْلَمُونَ ۝ ﴾

"...except for those who bear witness to the truth knowingly (i.e. believed in the Oneness of Allāh,

and obeyed His Orders), and they know." [*Sūrah az-Zukhruf* 43:86]

The commentators of the Qur'ān have said: "**who bear witness**" to *Lā Ilaha Illā-Allāh* (**none has the right to be worshipped in truth but Allāh**), "**and they know**" in their hearts the meaning of their testimony and they confess it with their tongues.

It has been reported on the authority of 'Uthman bin Affān (رَضِيَاللهُعَنهُ) that the Prophet (صَلَّىاللهُعَلَيهِوَسَلَّمَ) said:

مَنْ مَاتَ وَ هُوَ يَعْلَمُ أَنَّهُ لَا إِلَهَ إِلَّا اللهُ دَخَلَ الْجَنَّةَ

"**Whoever dies knowing (fully well) that none has the right to be worshipped in truth but Allāh enters Paradise.**"[24]

Thus, the Prophet (صَلَّىاللهُعَلَيهِوَسَلَّمَ) made knowledge a condition for this statement.

The second condition: <u>Certainty</u> (*al-Yaqīn*) that negates any doubt to an extent that the one who invokes this statement is firm with an unwavering belief. Certainty is the pinnacle of knowledge and its completeness. Allāh (سُبْحَانَهُوَتَعَالَى) said in describing the believers:

---

[24] Muslim; No. 26

"Only those are the believers who have believed in Allāh and His Messenger, and afterward doubt not but strive with their wealth and their lives for the Cause of Allāh. Those! They are the truthful." [*Sūrah al-Hujurāt* 49:15]

"**And afterward doubt not**" – meaning they had firm certainty without any doubt.

It has been reported on the authority of Abū Hurayrah (رَضِيَٱللَّهُعَنْهُ) that the Prophet (صَلَّىٱللَّهُعَلَيْهِوَسَلَّمَ) said:

أَشْهَدُ أَنْ لَا إِلَهَ إِلَّا اللهُ وَ أَنِّي رَسُولُ الله ، لَا يَلْقَى اللهَ بِهِمَا عَبْدٌ غَيْرُ شَاكٍّ فِيهِمَا إِلَّا دَخَلَ الْجَنَّةَ.

"I bear testimony to the fact that none has the right to be worshipped in truth but Allāh, and I am His messenger. The bondsman who would meet Allāh without entertaining any doubt about these (two fundamentals) would enter heaven."[25]

Also reported by the way of Abū Hurayrah (رَضِيَ ٱللَّهُ عَنْهُ), that the Prophet (صَلَّى ٱللَّهُ عَلَيْهِ وَسَلَّمَ) said:

مَنْ لَقِيتَ مِنْ وَرَاءِ الْحَائِطِ يَشْهَدُ أَنْ لَا إِلَهَ إِلَّا اللهُ مُسْتَيْقِناً بِهَا قَلْبُهُ ، فَبَشِّرْهُ بِالْجَنَّةِ.

"Whoever you meet outside this garden testifying that *Lā Ilaha Illā-Allāh* (none has the right to be worshipped in truth but Allāh), being assured of it in his heart, give him the glad tidings that he will enter Jannah." [26]

Thus marked for having certainty a condition for *Lā Ilaha Illā-Allāh*.

The Third Condition: Sincerity (*al-Ikhlās*) that negates polytheism and hypocrisy. This is achieved by purifying the deeds from all apparent and hidden deficiencies and having sincere intentions in all acts of worship for Allāh alone. Allāh (سُبْحَانَهُ وَتَعَالَى) said:

---

25 Muslim; No. 27
26 Sahih Muslim; No. 27.

﴿ أَلَا لِلَّهِ الدِّينُ الْخَالِصُ ﴾

"Surely the religion (i.e. the worship and the obedience) is for Allāh only." [*Sūrah az-Zumar* 39:3]

Moreover, He (سُبْحَانَهُوَتَعَالَى) said:

﴿ وَمَا أُمِرُوٓا۟ إِلَّا لِيَعْبُدُوا۟ اللَّهَ مُخْلِصِينَ لَهُ الدِّينَ ﴾

"And they were commanded not, but that they should worship Allāh, and worship none but Him Alone." [*Sūrah al-Bayyinah* 98:5]

In the authentic narration by Abū Hurayrah (رَضِيَٱللَّهُعَنْهُ), the Prophet (صَلَّىٱللَّهُعَلَيْهِوَسَلَّمَ) said:

أَسْعَدُ النَّاسِ بِشِفَاعَتِي: مَنْ قَالَ لَا إِلَهَ إِلَّا اللهُ ، خَالِصًا مِنْ قَلْبِهِ.

"The luckiest person who will have my intercession on the Day of Resurrection will be the one who said sincerely from the bottom of his heart "None has the right to be worshipped in truth but Allāh."

Thus considering sincerity yet another condition of *Lā Ilaha Illā-Allāh*.

The Forth Condition: Truthfulness (*as-Sidq*) that negates dishonesty. Therefore, one must invoke this statement truly from his heart. Truthfulness is compliance of the heart with the tongue. It is for the lack of such that Allāh ﷻ has reviled the hypocrites:

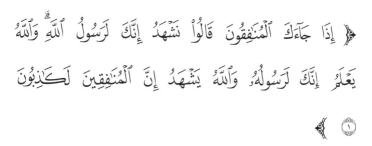

"When the hypocrites come to you (O Muhammad (ﷺ)), they say: "We bear witness that you are indeed the Messenger of Allāh." Allāh knows that you are indeed His Messenger, and Allāh bears witness that the hypocrites are liars indeed." [*Sūrah al-Munāfiqūn* 63:1]

So, He (سُبْحَانَهُوَتَعَالَى) described them as liars because the claim of their tongues is not present in their hearts. Moreover, Allāh (سُبْحَانَهُوَتَعَالَى) also said:

﴿ الٓمٓ ۞ أَحَسِبَ ٱلنَّاسُ أَن يُتْرَكُوٓاْ أَن يَقُولُوٓاْ ءَامَنَّا وَهُمْ لَا يُفْتَنُونَ ۞ وَلَقَدْ فَتَنَّا ٱلَّذِينَ مِن قَبْلِهِمْ فَلَيَعْلَمَنَّ ٱللَّهُ ٱلَّذِينَ صَدَقُواْ وَلَيَعْلَمَنَّ ٱلْكَٰذِبِينَ ۞ ﴾

"**Alif-Lâm-Mîm. Do people think that they will be left alone because they say: "We believe," and will not be tested.**" [*Sūrah al-Ankabūt* 29:1-3]

It has been reported by *Mu'ādh bin Jabal* (رَضِيَ ٱللَّهُ عَنْهُ) that the Prophet (صَلَّى ٱللَّهُ عَلَيْهِ وَسَلَّمَ) said:

مَا مِنْ أَحَدٍ يَشْهَدُ أَنْ لَا إِلَهَ إِلَّا اللهُ وَ أَنَّ مُحَمَّداً عَبْدُهُ وَ رَسُولُهُ صَادِقًا مِنْ قَلْبِهِ إِلَّا حَرَّمَهُ اللهُ عَلَى النَّارِ .

"**There is none who testifies truthfully that none has the right to be worshipped in truth but Allāh and Muhammad is his Apostle, except that Allāh, will save him from the Hell-fire**"[27].

---

[27] Al Bukhārī: No. 128, Muslim; No. 32

Hence, truthfulness is a required condition of *Lā Ilaha Illā-Allāh*.

The Fifth Condition: <u>Love</u> (*al-Mahabbah*) that negates hate and abomination. This is actualized by loving Allāh, His Messenger (ﷺ), Islām, and the Muslims who adhere to the obedience of Allāh, as well as disapproving anyone who goes against *Lā Ilaha Illā-Allāh* and commits any of its nullifiers of polytheism or disbelief. As for the proof for making love one of the conditions, it is the statement of Allāh (سُبْحَانَهُوَتَعَالَى):

﴿ وَمِنَ ٱلنَّاسِ مَن يَتَّخِذُ مِن دُونِ ٱللَّهِ أَندَادًا يُحِبُّونَهُمْ كَحُبِّ ٱللَّهِ وَٱلَّذِينَ ءَامَنُوٓا۟ أَشَدُّ حُبًّا لِّلَّهِ ﴾

"**And of mankind are some who take (for worship) others besides Allāh as rivals (to Allāh). They love them as they love Allāh. But those who believe, love Allāh more (than anything else).**"
[*Sūrah al-Baqarah* 2:165]

And the *hadīth* from the Prophet (ﷺ) where he stated:

أَوْثَقُ عُرَى الْإِيمَانِ الْحُبُّ فِي اللهِ وَالْبُغْضُ

"The most stronghold of *Īmān* (faith) is to love in the cause of Allāh and to hate in the cause of Allāh (i.e. disprove of anything displeasing to Him)."[28]

The Sixth Condition: Acceptance (*al-Qubūl*) that negates rejection. It is a must to fully and wholeheartedly accept this statement and all that it entails. Indeed, the Qur'ān narrates the tales of those whom Allāh spared their destruction for embracing *Lā Ilaha Illā-Allāh*, and the destruction of those that rejected it. Allāh (سُبْحَانَهُوَتَعَالَى) says:

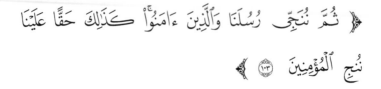

"Then (in the end) We save Our Messengers and those who believe! Thus it is incumbent upon Us to save the believers." [*Sūrah Yūnus* 10:103]

Allāh (سُبْحَانَهُوَتَعَالَى) said regarding the idol worshippers:

---

[28] Ahmad in the Musnad 4/286

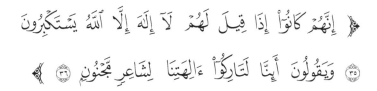

﴿ إِنَّهُمْ كَانُوٓا۟ إِذَا قِيلَ لَهُمْ لَآ إِلَٰهَ إِلَّا ٱللَّهُ يَسْتَكْبِرُونَ ﴾

﴿ وَيَقُولُونَ أَئِنَّا لَتَارِكُوٓا۟ ءَالِهَتِنَا لِشَاعِرٍ مَّجْنُونٍ ﴿٣٦﴾ ﴾ (٣٥)

"Truly, when it was said to them: *Lā Ilaha Illā-Allāh* they puffed themselves up with pride (i.e. denied it). And (they) said: "Are we going to abandon our ālihah (gods) for the sake of a mad poet?" [*Sūrah a-Sāffāt* 37:35-36]

The Seventh condition: <u>Submission</u> (*al-Inqiyād*) and Compliance that negates neglect. For it is a must upon anyone invoking *Lā Ilaha Illā-Allāh* to adhere to the legislations of Allāh, follow His commands, and submit entirely to Him. Allāh (سُبْحَانَهُوَتَعَالَى) says:

﴿ ۞ وَمَن يُسْلِمْ وَجْهَهُۥٓ إِلَى ٱللَّهِ وَهُوَ مُحْسِنٌ فَقَدِ ٱسْتَمْسَكَ بِٱلْعُرْوَةِ ٱلْوُثْقَىٰ ﴾

"And whosoever submits his face (himself) to Allāh, while he is a Muhsin (good-doer), then he has grasped the most trustworthy handhold." [*Sūrah Luqmān* 31:22]

"**Trustworthy handhold.**" means holding to *Lā Ilaha Illā-Allāh*. So, Allāh has made submission and compliance (to the religious legislation) a condition of this statement.

These are the conditions of *Lā Ilaha Illā-Allāh*. The intent here is not to merely count them and memorize them, rather to fulfill and adhere to them. Although many common people are unable to name these conditions, they abide by them and commit their lives to its values. On the other hand, some excel in naming these conditions, yet fail to uphold them and often fall into their nullifiers. The intent, therefore, is the combination of knowledge and fulfillment. Thus, seek to be amongst the true people of *Lā Ilaha Illā-Allāh*, and part of the fellowship of *Tawhīd*. We ask Allāh (سُبْحَانَهُ وَتَعَالَى) to grant us success in fulfilling that, and assistance in maintaining firmness.

THE SIGNIFICANCE OF THE WORD OF *TAWHĪD: LĀ ILAHA ILLĀ-ALLĀH*

The most virtuous of words - the word of *Tawhīd- Lā Ilaha Illā-Allāh*- will not be accepted by mere utterance of the tongue. Rather, an implementation of its fundamental principles is necessary. For example, disproving polytheism and affirming the oneness of Allāh with a firm belief and adherence to all that it entails. This is the only way can anyone be considered a Muslim or be in the fold of the people of *Tawhīd (Lā Ilaha Illā-Allāh)*. This great word signifies the falsehood of any deity besides Allāh. To affirm any deity other than Allāh is the most atrocious aggression and most evil deviation. Allāh (سُبْحَانَهُوَتَعَالَى) says:

﴿ وَمَنْ أَضَلُّ مِمَّن يَدْعُواْ مِن دُونِ ٱللَّهِ مَن لَّا
يَسْتَجِيبُ لَهُۥ إِلَىٰ يَوْمِ ٱلْقِيَٰمَةِ وَهُمْ عَن دُعَآئِهِمْ غَٰفِلُونَ
۝ وَإِذَا حُشِرَ ٱلنَّاسُ كَانُواْ لَهُمْ أَعْدَآءً وَكَانُواْ بِعِبَادَتِهِمْ كَٰفِرِينَ ﴾
۝

"Say: "Think you about all that you invoke besides Allāh? Show me. What have they created of the earth? Or have they a share in (the creation of) the heavens? Bring me a Book (revealed before this), or some trace of knowledge (in support of your claims), if you are truthful!. And who is more astray than one who calls on (invokes) besides Allāh, such as will not answer him till the Day of Resurrection, and who are (even) unaware of their calls (invocations) to them?" [*Sūrah al-Ahqāf* 46:5-6]

And Allāh (سُبْحَانَهُوَتَعَالَى) says:

$$﴿ ذَٰلِكَ بِأَنَّ ٱللَّهَ هُوَ ٱلْحَقُّ وَأَنَّ مَا يَدْعُونَ مِن دُونِهِۦ هُوَ ٱلْبَـٰطِلُ وَأَنَّ ٱللَّهَ هُوَ ٱلْعَلِيُّ ٱلْكَبِيرُ ٦٢ ﴾$$

"That is because Allāh - He is the Truth (the only True God of all that exists, Who has no partners or rivals with Him), and what they (the polytheists) invoke besides Him, it is Bātil (falsehood). And verily, Allāh - He is the Most High, the Most Great." [*Sūrah al-Hajj* 22:26]

Also, Allāh (سُبْحَانَهُوَتَعَالَى) says:

$$﴿ إِنَّ ٱلشِّرْكَ لَظُلْمٌ عَظِيمٌ ١٣ ﴾$$

"Verily joining others in worship with Allāh is a great Dhûlm (wrong) indeed." [*Sūrah Luqmān* 31:13]

And Allāh (سُبْحَانَهُوَتَعَالَى) says:

﴿ وَٱلۡكَٰفِرُونَ هُمُ ٱلظَّٰلِمُونَ ۝ ﴾

"And it is the disbelievers who are the Dhālimūn (wrong-doers)." [*Sūrah al-Baqarah* 2:254]

Oppression (*dhulm*) is misplacing anything from its rightful place. Therefore, directing any act of worship to other than Allāh is a form of oppression; the most severe kind since, it is a displacement of a right which is due only to Allāh.

The meaning of *Lā Ilaha Illā-Allāh* must be comprehended and fully understood since the mere invocation, apart from full grasp and implementation, has no benefit according to the consensus of the scholars of Islam. Allāh (سُبْحَانَهُوَتَعَالَى) says:

﴿ وَلَا يَمۡلِكُ ٱلَّذِينَ يَدۡعُونَ مِن دُونِهِ ٱلشَّفَٰعَةَ إِلَّا مَن شَهِدَ بِٱلۡحَقِّ وَهُمۡ يَعۡلَمُونَ ۝ ﴾

"And those whom they invoke instead of Him have no power of intercession - except for those who bear witness to the truth knowingly and they know." [*Sūrah al-Ahqāf* 46:86]

Commentators of the Qur'ān noted the verse "and they know" to mean: Except anyone who testifies with *Lā Ilaha Illā-Allāh* while knowing in the heart what is uttered on the tongue. The reason being, is that a testimony necessitates knowledge, for if it were out of ignorance, it will not be considered a testimony.

By knowledge the person will be saved from the way of the Christians; acting on deeds without concrete knowledge. By implementation and adherence, the person will be guarded from the ways of the Jews; possessing knowledge while not acting upon it. Finally, with honesty, the person will be spared the way of the hypocrites; revealing outwardly something different from what is concealed in the heart. Thereby, the person will be amongst the people of the straight path of Allāh; the way of those on whom He has bestowed His Grace, not the way of those who earned His Anger, nor of those who went astray.

In all, *Lā Ilaha Illā-Allāh*- the word of *Tawhīd*- will only benefit whoever recognizes its significance, understands its meaning, believes it firmly, and upholds its principles. As for whoever implores it, while only adhering to it outwardly without belief, then they are a hypocrite. Likewise whoever claims *Lā Ilaha Illā-Allāh*, yet engages in deeds contrary to its principles and negates it with polytheism is a disbeliever. Also, it will not benefit the one that invokes *Lā Ilaha Illā-Allāh* and apostates from Islām by denying any of its underlying principles, even if he were to utter it a thousand times. Likewise is the one that invokes this word while directing some acts of worship (i.e. Prayer, slaughtering, repentance, and reliance) to other than Allāh. In such cases, mere invocation will not be sufficient, nor will it bring benefit due to what has been neglected from the necessity of monotheism and sincerity; the core of the great word of *Tawhīd*.

Lā Ilaha Illā-Allāh means there is no deity worthy of worship except the one true God; Allāh, alone without any partners. *Ilāh* linguistically means the worshiped one. Therefore, *Lā Ilaha Illā-Allāh* means there is no one worthy of worship in truth but Allāh. Allāh (سُبْحَانَهُوَتَعَالَى) said:

$$﴿ وَمَآ أَرْسَلْنَا مِن قَبْلِكَ مِن رَّسُولٍ إِلَّا نُوحِىٓ إِلَيْهِ أَنَّهُۥ لَآ إِلَٰهَ إِلَّآ أَنَا۠ فَٱعْبُدُونِ ۝ ﴾$$

"And We did not send any Messenger before you (O Muhammad (ﷺ)) but We revealed to him (saying): Lā Ilāh Illā Ana [none has the right to be worshipped in truth but I (Allāh)], so worship Me (Alone and none else)." [*Sūrah al-Anbiyā'* 21:25]

Similarly, Allāh (سُبْحَانَهُ وَتَعَالَى) said:

﴿ وَلَقَدْ بَعَثْنَا فِى كُلِّ أُمَّةٍ رَسُولًا أَنِ اعْبُدُواْ اللَّهَ وَاجْتَنِبُواْ الطَّاغُوتَ ﴾

"And verily, We have sent among every Ummah (community, nation) a Messenger (proclaiming): "Worship Allāh (Alone), and avoid (or keep away from) Tāghūt (all false deities i.e. do not worship Tāghūt besides Allāh)." [*Sūrah an-Nahl* 16:36]

Hence, it becomes clear that *Ilāh* does indeed mean the worshiped one. Then *Lā Ilaha Illā-Allāh* means to single out Allāh alone for all acts of worship and to abstain from *Tāghūt*. For that reason, when the Messenger (ﷺ) said to the disbelievers of Quraysh: "Say *Lā Ilaha Illā-Allāh*!" they replied;

﴿ أَجَعَلَ ٱلْأَلِهَةَ إِلَٰهًا وَٰحِدًا إِنَّ هَٰذَا لَشَىْءٌ عُجَابٌ ۝ ﴾

"Has he made the ālihah (gods) (all) into One Ilāh (God - Allāh). Verily, this is a curious thing! "[*Sūrah Sād* 38:5]

And the people of Hūd said to their Messenger:

﴿ أَجِئْتَنَا لِنَعْبُدَ ٱللَّهَ وَحْدَهُ وَنَذَرَ مَا كَانَ يَعْبُدُ ءَابَآؤُنَا ﴾

"You have come to us that we should worship Allāh Alone and forsake that which our fathers used to worship. " [*Sūrah al-A'rāf* 7:70]

The above reply was in response to the call to *Lā Ilaha Illā-Allāh,* which was due to their understanding of it to mean banishing divinity from their idols and anything other than Allāh.

The word *Lā Ilaha Illā-Allāh* is composed of negation and affirmation. It negates any form of divinity from all besides Allāh, including the angels and the Messengers, and affirming divinity to Allāh alone. Thus, the servant ought to seek Allāh alone, attaching their heart and turning to Him in worship . The Qur'ān contains many verses that portray the meaning of the word of *Tawhīd: Lā Ilaha Illā-Allāh*, and clarify its purpose. For example, Allāh (سُبْحَانَهُوَتَعَالَى) said:

"And your Ilāh (God) is One Ilāh (God - Allāh), Lā Ilāha Illā Huwa (there is none who has the right to be worshipped in truth but He), the Most Gracious, the Most Merciful." [*Sūrah al-Baqarah* 2:163]

Also Allāh (سُبْحَانَهُوَتَعَالَى) said:

﴿ وَمَا أُمِرُوٓاْ إِلَّا لِيَعْبُدُواْ ٱللَّهَ مُخْلِصِينَ لَهُ ٱلدِّينَ حُنَفَآءَ ﴾

"And they were commanded not, but that they should worship Allāh, and worship none but Him Alone." [*Sūrah al-Bayyinah* 98:5]

Also,

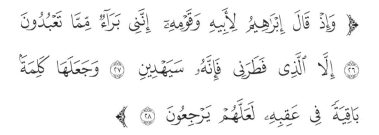

"And (remember) when Ibrāhīm (Abraham) said to his father and his people: "Verily, I am innocent of what you worship, "Except Him (i.e. I worship none but Allāh Alone) Who did create me; and verily He will guide me." And he made it [i.e. *Lā Ilaha Illā-Allāh* (none has the right to be worshipped in truth but Allāh Alone)] a Word lasting among his offspring, (True Monotheism), that they may turn back." [*Sūrah az-Zukhruf* 43:26-28]

Allāh (سُبْحَانَهُوَتَعَالَى) said in narrating the story of the believer in chapter Yāsīn:

﴿ وَمَا لِیَ لَا أَعْبُدُ ٱلَّذِی فَطَرَنِی وَإِلَیْهِ تُرْجَعُونَ ۝ ءَأَتَّخِذُ مِن دُونِهِ ءَالِهَةً إِن يُرِدْنِ ٱلرَّحْمَٰنُ بِضُرٍّ لَّا تُغْنِ عَنِّی شَفَٰعَتُهُمْ شَیْئًا وَلَا يُنقِذُونِ ۝ إِنِّی إِذًا لَّفِی ضَلَٰلٍ مُّبِينٍ ۝ ﴾

"And why should I not worship Him (Allāh Alone) Who has created me and to Whom you shall be returned. "Shall I take besides Him ālihah (gods)? If the Most Gracious (Allāh) intends me any harm, their intercession will be of no use for me whatsoever, nor can they save me?" [*Sūrah Yāsīn* 36:22-24]

And Allāh (سُبْحَانَهُوَتَعَالَى) said:

﴾ قُلْ إِنِّى أُمِرْتُ أَنْ أَعْبُدَ ٱللَّهَ مُخْلِصًا لَّهُ ٱلدِّينَ ۝ وَأُمِرْتُ لِأَنْ أَكُونَ أَوَّلَ ٱلْمُسْلِمِينَ ۝ قُلْ إِنِّى أَخَافُ إِنْ عَصَيْتُ رَبِّى عَذَابَ يَوْمٍ عَظِيمٍ ۝ قُلِ ٱللَّهَ أَعْبُدُ مُخْلِصًا لَّهُ دِينِى ۝ ﴿

"Say (O Muhammad (صَلَّىٱللَّهُعَلَيْهِوَسَلَّمَ)): "Verily I am commanded to worship Allāh (Alone) by obeying Him and doing religious deeds sincerely for His sake only. "And I am commanded (this) in order that I may be the first of those who submit themselves to Allāh (in Islâm) as Muslims." Say (O Muhammad (صَلَّىٱللَّهُعَلَيْهِوَسَلَّمَ)): "Verily if I disobey my Lord, I am afraid of the torment of a great Day." Say (O Muhammad (صَلَّىٱللَّهُعَلَيْهِوَسَلَّمَ)): "Allāh Alone I worship by doing religious deeds sincerely for His sake only (and

not to show off, and not to set up rivals with Him in worship.).” [*Sūrah az-Zumar* 39:11-14]

And Allāh (سُبْحَانَهُوَتَعَالَى) said about the believer of Fir'awn's household:

﴿ ۞ وَيَٰقَوۡمِ مَا لِىٓ أَدۡعُوكُمۡ إِلَى ٱلنَّجَوٰةِ وَتَدۡعُونَنِىٓ إِلَى ٱلنَّارِ ۝ تَدۡعُونَنِى لِأَكۡفُرَ بِٱللَّهِ وَأُشۡرِكَ بِهِۦ مَا لَيۡسَ لِى بِهِۦ عِلۡمٌ وَأَنَا۠ أَدۡعُوكُمۡ إِلَى ٱلۡعَزِيزِ ٱلۡغَفَّٰرِ ۝ لَا جَرَمَ أَنَّمَا تَدۡعُونَنِىٓ إِلَيۡهِ لَيۡسَ لَهُۥ دَعۡوَةٌ فِى ٱلدُّنۡيَا وَلَا فِى ٱلۡأَخِرَةِ وَأَنَّ مَرَدَّنَآ إِلَى ٱللَّهِ وَأَنَّ ٱلۡمُسۡرِفِينَ هُمۡ أَصۡحَٰبُ ٱلنَّارِ ۝ ﴾

“And O my people! How is it that I call you to salvation while you call me to the Fire! “You invite me to disbelieve in Allāh (and in His Oneness), and to join partners in worship with Him of which I have no knowledge; and I invite you to the All-Mighty, the Oft-Forgiving! “No doubt you call me to (worship) one who cannot grant (me) my request (or respond to my invocation) in this world or in the Hereafter. And our return will be to Allāh, and *al-Musrifūn* (i.e. polytheists and arrogant ones, those who commit great sins, the transgressors of Allāh's set limits):

they shall be the dwellers of the Fire! "[*Sūrah Ghāfir* 40:41-43]

And the verses to this effect are plenty in number in the Qur'ān. All of verses point to the same meaning, which is to be free from worshipping other than Allāh (i.e. Idols, intercessors, etc.). Instead, single out Allāh for all acts of worship. That is the guidance and true religion which Allāh has sent with the Prophets and contained in the scriptures. It does not suffice to invoke *Lā Ilaha Illā-Allāh* without a firm grasp of its meaning or implementation of its principles. Conceivably, one may direct to other than Allāh an act of worship that is only due to Allāh alone.

In conclusion, the word of *Tawhīd* is not a meaningless phrase, baseless notion, or empty words. Some may wrongly conceive the purpose of this word to be merely uttered on the tongue with complete detachment of belief in the heart or implementation of the limbs. Rather, it encompasses great pertinence and magnificent meaning as previously clarified: turning to Allāh in submission, humility, and reliance of Him and utter disbelief of all that is worshiped other than Him.

Such a lofty word and crystal clear matter. However, the success to guidance is in the hands of Allāh, and we seek His assistance.

THE NULLIFIERS OF THE TESTIMONY: *LĀ ILAHA ILLĀ-ALLĀH*

We have previously discussed in detail the conditions of *Lā Ilaha Illā-Allāh* that each Muslim must establish to validate the deeds. Conditions that are of great importance and hold high status, which requires each Muslim to uphold and dedicate great care and concern. In equal importance, the Muslim- in this regard- must be aware of the nullifiers of this word, so as to be cautious of them.

Indeed in the Qur'ān, Allāh has clarified in great detail the path of the believers who fulfilled *Lā Ilaha Illā-Allāh*; their deeds, means of success, outcome and returning place. Similarly, the Qur'ān details the path of the wrongdoers; their deeds, causes of their doom, and awaiting punishment. The Qur'ān sheds light on the affairs of both groups, leaving nothing concealed. Allāh (سُبْحَانَهُ وَتَعَالَى) said:

﴿ وَكَذَلِكَ نُفَصِّلُ ٱلْأَيَتِ وَلِتَسْتَبِينَ سَبِيلُ ٱلْمُجْرِمِينَ ﴾

"And thus do We explain the Ayāt (proofs, evidence, verses, lessons, signs, revelations, etc.) in detail, that the way of the Mujrimūn (criminals, polytheists, sinners) may become manifest." [*Sūrah al-Anām* 6:55]

And Allāh (سُبْحَانَهُوَتَعَالَى) also said:

﴿ وَمَن يُشَاقِقِ ٱلرَّسُولَ مِنۢ بَعْدِ مَا تَبَيَّنَ لَهُ ٱلْهُدَىٰ وَيَتَّبِعْ غَيْرَ سَبِيلِ ٱلْمُؤْمِنِينَ نُوَلِّهِۦ مَا تَوَلَّىٰ وَنُصْلِهِۦ جَهَنَّمَ وَسَآءَتْ مَصِيرًا ۝ ﴾

"And whoever contradicts and opposes the Messenger (Muhammad (صَلَّىٱللَّهُعَلَيْهِوَسَلَّمَ)) after the right path has been shown clearly to him, and follows other than the believers' way, We shall keep him in the path he has chosen, and burn him in Hell - what an evil destination!" [*Sūrah an-Nisā'* 4:115]

Whoever is unaware of the affairs of the wrongdoers will always be on the verge of falling victim to some of their falsehood. '*Umar bin Khattab* (رَضِيَٱللَّهُعَنْهُ) said:

إِنَّمَا تُنْقَضُ عُرَى الْإِسْلَامِ عُرْوَةً عُرْوَةً، إِذَا نَشَأَ فِي
الْإِسْلَامِ مَنْ لَمْ يَعْرِفِ الْجَاهِلِيَّةَ

**"The knots of Islām (i.e. strongly held principles)
will be undone knot by knot once found in Islām
people that do not know of the Ignorance period
(period prior to Islām)."** [29]

Consequently, numerous verses of the Qur'ān and texts
of the *Sunnah* dedicate a great effort to warn against all
matters that lead to apostasy or disbelief that negates the
word of *Tawhīd: Lā Ilaha Illā-Allāh.* Similarly, the Islāmic
scholars note in the books of jurisprudence (*Fiqh*) under
the heading of "The ruling of apostasy" that there are
many nullifiers that cause a Muslim to apostate. In other
word, any Muslim who commits such nullifiers leaves
the fold of Islām. In such case, the mere invocation of *Lā
Ilaha Illā-Allāh* does no benefit. Reason being that the
word of *Tawhīd* can only be valid and beneficial when
the conditions are established and the nullifiers are
avoided.

Undoubtedly, there are a lot of benefits for the Muslim
in knowing these nullifiers; especially when the goal of

---

[29] *Al-Fawā'id* by Ibn Qayyim, p. 201 and on.

knowing them is to seek salvation and caution from the evil. Benefits include an increase of apprehension and love of the Truth, a sense of clarity, safeguarding of one's faith from any fault, and cautioning others of this evil. Besides, Allāh loves the path of truth to be known and pursued, while the paths of falsehood to be exposed and guarded against. Therefore, the Muslim is obligated to know the path of good and follow it and have awareness of the path of evil and abstain from it. *Hudaifah ibn Yamān* (رَضِيَٱللَّهُعَنْهُ) said,

كَانَ الصَّحَابَةُ يَسْأَلُونَ رَسُولَ الله صَلَّى اللهُ عَلَيْهِ عَنِ الْخَيْرِ، وَ كُنْتُ أَسْأَلُهُ عَنِ الشَّرِّ مَخَافَةَ أَنْ يُدْرِكَنِي .

"The people used to ask Allāh's Messenger (صَلَّىٱللَّهُعَلَيْهِوَسَلَّمَ) about the good but I used to ask him about the evil lest I should be overtaken by them."[30]

And for this reason it was stated,

وَ لَكِنْ لِتَوَقِّيهِ   عَرَفْتُ الشَّرَّ لَا لِلشَّرِّ

---

[30] Al Bukhari 3606, Muslim No. 1847

وَ مَنْ لَا يَعْرِفِ الـشَّـرَّ   مِنَ النَّـاسِ يَـقَعْ فِيـهِ

"I learned about evil not to commit it, rather to protect myself from it. So whoever does not learn about evil will certainly fall into it."

Considering the importance of the matter, it becomes an obligation on each Muslim to know the nullifiers of *Lā Ilaha Illā-Allāh*. As preceded, the nullifiers are plenty in number, however the most severe and most common amongst them are ten- as noted by the scholars. The following is a concise for the Muslim to be cautions of and caution other Muslims.

The first: to join partners with Allāh (polytheism) in the acts of worship. Allāh (سُبْحَانَهُوَتَعَالَى) says:

﴿ إِنَّ ٱللَّهَ لَا يَغْفِرُ أَن يُشْرَكَ بِهِۦ وَيَغْفِرُ مَا دُونَ ذَٰلِكَ لِمَن يَشَآءُ وَمَن يُشْرِكْ بِٱللَّهِ فَقَدْ ضَلَّ ضَلَٰلًا بَعِيدًا ﴿١١٦﴾ ﴾

"Verily! Allāh forgives not (the sin of) setting up partners (in worship) with Him, but He forgives whom He wills sins other than that, and whoever sets up partners in worship with Allāh, has indeed strayed far away." [*Sūrah an-Nisā'* 4:116]

And He (سُبْحَانَهُوَتَعَالَى) said:

﴿ إِنَّهُۥ مَن يُشۡرِكۡ بِٱللَّهِ فَقَدۡ حَرَّمَ ٱللَّهُ عَلَيۡهِ ٱلۡجَنَّةَ وَمَأۡوَىٰهُ ٱلنَّارُ وَمَا لِلظَّٰلِمِينَ مِنۡ أَنصَارٍ ۝ ﴾

"Verily, whosoever sets up partners (in worship) with Allāh, then Allāh has forbidden Paradise to him, and the Fire will be his abode. And for the Zâlimûn (polytheists and wrong-doers) there are no helpers." [*Sūrah al-Mā'idah* 5:72]

This also includes the calling upon the dead to seek assistance, slaughter for them, etc.

The second: whoever takes intermediates between him and Allāh; to call upon them, seek intercession, and rely on them, has disbelieved by the consensus of the scholars. Allāh (سُبْحَانَهُوَتَعَالَى) said:

﴿ وَيَعۡبُدُونَ مِن دُونِ ٱللَّهِ مَا لَا يَضُرُّهُمۡ وَلَا يَنفَعُهُمۡ وَيَقُولُونَ هَٰٓؤُلَآءِ شُفَعَٰٓؤُنَا عِندَ ٱللَّهِ قُلۡ أَتُنَبِّئُونَ ٱللَّهَ بِمَا لَا يَعۡلَمُ فِي ٱلسَّمَٰوَٰتِ وَلَا فِي ٱلۡأَرۡضِ سُبۡحَٰنَهُۥ وَتَعَٰلَىٰ عَمَّا يُشۡرِكُونَ ۝ ﴾

"And they worship besides Allāh things that
harm them not, nor profit them, and they say:
"These are our intercessors with Allāh." Say: "Do
you inform Allāh of that which He knows not in
the heavens and on the earth?" Glorified and
Exalted is He above all that which they associate
as partners (with Him)!" [*Sūrah Yūnus* 10:18]

The third: whoever does not hold the polytheists to be
disbeliever, doubts their disbelief, or validates their
religion has indeed disbelieved.

The forth: whoever believes that guidance and a path
other than that of the Prophet (ﷺ) is more
complete, or favors others over his judgment- has
disbelieved; in the same scale as favoring the ruling of
the wrongdoers over the ruling of Allāh.

The fifth: whoever abominates anything legislated by
the Prophet (ﷺ) regardless of acting upon it or
not, has disbelieved. Allāh (سُبْحَانَهُوَتَعَالَى) said:

﴿ ذَٰلِكَ بِأَنَّهُمْ كَرِهُوا۟ مَآ أَنزَلَ ٱللَّهُ فَأَحْبَطَ أَعْمَٰلَهُمْ ۝ ﴾

"That is because they hate that which Allāh has
sent down (this Qur'ān and Islāmic laws, etc.); so

He has made their deeds fruitless." [*Sūrah Muhammad* 47:9]

The sixth: whoever makes mockery of the religion of the Prophet (ﷺ) (Islām), or the rewards and punishments thereof, has disbelieved. Allāh (سُبْحَانَهُ وَتَعَالَى) said:

﴿ قُلْ أَبِٱللَّهِ وَءَايَٰتِهِۦ وَرَسُولِهِۦ كُنتُمْ تَسْتَهْزِءُونَ ۝ لَا تَعْتَذِرُواْ قَدْ كَفَرْتُم بَعْدَ إِيمَٰنِكُمْ إِن نَّعْفُ عَن طَآئِفَةٍ مِّنكُمْ نُعَذِّبْ طَآئِفَةَۢ بِأَنَّهُمْ كَانُواْ مُجْرِمِينَ ۝ ﴾

"Say: "Was it at Allāh (عَزَّوَجَلَّ), and His Ayāt (verses, signs, revelations) and His Messenger (ﷺ) that you were mocking? Make no excuse; you disbelieved after you had believed. If We pardon some of you, We will punish others amongst you because they were Mujrimūn (disbelievers, polytheists, sinners, criminals.)." [*Sūrah at-Tawbah* 9:65-66]

The seventh: Sorcery, which includes magic spells that causes a person to hate (*sarf*) or love (`atf*) someone/something. So whoever performs it or is pleased with it being done, has disbelieved. Allāh (سُبْحَانَهُ وَتَعَالَى) said:

﴿ وَمَا يُعَلِّمَانِ مِنْ أَحَدٍ حَتَّىٰ يَقُولَا إِنَّمَا نَحْنُ فِتْنَةٌ فَلَا تَكْفُرْ ﴾

"Neither of these two (angels) taught anyone (such things) till they had said, "We are only for trial, so disbelieve not (by learning this magic from us)." [*Sūrah al-Baqarah* 2:102]

The eighth: Supporting and assisting the polytheists against the Muslims. Allāh (سُبْحَانَهُ وَتَعَالَى) said:

﴿ وَمَن يَتَوَلَّهُم مِّنكُمْ فَإِنَّهُۥ مِنْهُمْ إِنَّ ٱللَّهَ لَا يَهْدِى ٱلْقَوْمَ ٱلظَّٰلِمِينَ ﴾ (٥١)

"And if any amongst you takes them (as Awliyā' - helpers), then surely he is one of them. Verily, Allāh guides not those people who are the Zālimūn (polytheists and wrong-doers and unjust)." [*Sūrah al-Mā'idah* 5:51]

The ninth: Whoever believes that it is permitted for some people to be free of (implementing) the legislation of the Prophet

(صَلَّى ٱللَّهُ عَلَيْهِ وَسَلَّمَ) (i.e. Islām), then he is a disbeliever. Allāh (سُبْحَانَهُ وَتَعَالَى) said:

$$\text{﴿ وَمَن يَبْتَغِ غَيْرَ ٱلْإِسْلَٰمِ دِينًا فَلَن يُقْبَلَ مِنْهُ وَهُوَ فِى ٱلْأَخِرَةِ مِنَ ٱلْخَٰسِرِينَ ۝ ﴾}$$

"And whoever seeks a religion other than Islâm, it will never be accepted of him, and in the Hereafter he will be one of the losers." [*Sūrah Āli 'Imrān* 3:85]

The Tenth: Turning away from Allāh's Religion, not learning it or Implementing it (is an act of disbelief). Allāh (سُبْحَانَهُ وَتَعَالَى) said:

$$\text{﴿ وَمَنْ أَظْلَمُ مِمَّن ذُكِّرَ بِآيَٰتِ رَبِّهِ ثُمَّ أَعْرَضَ عَنْهَآ إِنَّا مِنَ ٱلْمُجْرِمِينَ مُنتَقِمُونَ ۝ ﴾}$$

"And who does wronger than he who is reminded of the Ayāt (proofs, evidence, verses, lessons, signs, revelations, etc.) of his Lord, then turns aside from that? Verily, We shall exact retribution from the *Mujrimūn* (criminals, disbelievers, polytheists, sinners)." [*Sūrah a-Sajdah* 32:22]

So, these are ten of the nullifiers of the word of *Tawhīd*. Whoever commits any of it- we seek refuge in Allāh from such – has nullified his *Tawhīd*, ruined his faith, and the invocation of *Lā Ilaha Illā-Allāh* is of no benefit to him. The scholars of Islām make no distinction concerning committing any of these nullifiers, between the one who jokes, the one who is serious or the one who does so out of fear. However, the one who commits   them   due to being coerced is excused. All of these (ten) matters are from the gravest in danger and from those   that   most   often   occur.   So   the Muslim must beware of them and fear from these acts befalling him.

THE INVALIDITY OF SUPPLICATING ONLY WITH THE SINGULAR NOUN OF PRONOUN OF "ALLĀH"

The discussion has been – thus far – regarding the virtues of the word of *Tawhīd*. As stated, it is the best supplication and most simple of phrases, yet greatest in meaning and benefit. The need of the people for this word is the most essential of needs. Greater than the need of food, drink, clothing, and the rest of their affairs. As such, it is the most widely used supplication, most easily attained, greatest in meaning and highest of status.

Despite such virtue and prestige, some of the common and ignorant people deviate from the word of *Tawhīd* to innovated supplications and invented prayers which have no basis in the Qur'ān and the *Sunnah* nor has any trace to the righteous predecessors. An example of such is the customs of the factions of the Sufi sect; in particular, the supplications. They supplicate with only the singular noun of "Allāh, Allāh" in repetition. Some, even suffice with the pronoun "He, He" (i.e. referring to Allāh) repeated over and over. In extreme factions, the word of *Tawhīd* is said to be for the common folk Muslims, the singular noun "Allāh" is the distinguished worshipers, and the pronoun "He" for the high ranking amongst the distinguished. In doing so, they favor supplicating with the singular noun and the pronoun over the word of *Tawhīd;* a word which the Prophet (ﷺ) considered to be the most virtuous supplication and the best phrase uttered by all the Messengers.

Furthermore, there is no legislation text of Qur'ān verse or excerpt from the *Sunnah* that supports or validates such form of supplication. It is mere invention of some contemporary wrongdoers. The renown Islāmic scholar *Ibn Taymiyyah* (رحمه الله) has disproved the claims of those sects in this matter. He proved the invalidity of their supporting arguments and textual evidence.

In a quote, he said:

> **"Conceivably, some of their authors might discuss the exaltation of such supplication, which often times are derived from either inspiration or sheer assumption or reported *hadith*. As for the reported *hadith*, they hold the narration stating that the Prophet (ﷺ) dictated to 'Ali bin Abi Tālib (رضي الله عنه) to say "Allāh, Allāh, Allāh". The Prophet (ﷺ) said it three times and commanded 'Ali to say it three times. This narration, however, is a fabrication**

on the consensus of the scholars of *hadith*. Rather, the affirmed narration is the dictation of the Prophet (ﷺ) of the word of *Tawhīd*, especially as he (ﷺ) pleaded to his uncle to say it as he was on the deathbed:

يَا عَمِّ ، قُلْ : لَا إِلَهَ إِلَّا اللهُ ، كَلِمَةً أُحَاجُّ لَكَ بِهَا عِنْدَ اللهِ .

"O my uncle! Say: None has the right to be worshipped except Allāh, an expression I will defend your case with, before Allāh."[31]

The Prophet (ﷺ) also said,

إِنِّي لَأَعْلَمُ كَلِمَةً لَا يَقُولُهَا عَبْدٌ عِنْدَ الْمَوْتِ إِلَّا وَجَدَ رُوحَهُ لَهَا رَوْحًا

"I know a word which no one says at the time of death but his soul will find comfort"[32],

And he said,

---

[31] Al Bukhari No. 3884; Muslim No. 24
[32] Ahmad in Musnad 1/28, Ibn Maajah No. 3795

مَنْ كَانَ آخِرَ كَلَامِهِ لَا إِلَهَ إِلَّا اللهُ دَخَلَ الْجَنَّةَ .

**"He whose last words are: `Lā Ilaha Illā-Allāh'
(none has the right to be worshipped in truth but
Allāh) will enter Jannah."**[33]

Also he said,

أُمِرْتُ أَنْ أُقَاتِلَ النَّاسَ حَتَّى يَشْهَدُوا أَنْ لَا إِلَهَ إِلَّا اللهُ

وَ أَنَّ مُحَمَّداً رَسُولُ الله ، فَإِذَا فَعَلُوا ذَلِكَ ، عَصَمُوا

مِنِّي دِمَاءَهُمْ وَ أَمْوَالَهُمْ إِلَّا بِحَقِّهَا وَ حِسَابُهُمْ

عَلَى الله .

**"I have been commanded (by Allāh) to fight
people until they testify that there is no true god
except Allāh, and that Muhammad is the
Messenger of Allāh, and perform Salat and pay
Zakat. If they do so, they will have protection of
their blood and property from me except when
justified by Islām, and then account is left to
Allāh."**

---

[33] Ahmad in Musnad 5/247, Abu Dawud No. 3116. Rated as Hasan
by Albany

This is only a few of many narrations related to the topic.

Supplication with the singular noun "Allāh" has not been legislated under any circumstance. Likewise, there is nothing to show the permissibility of such in the sources of the religion. However, there is an illusion that some devout worshipers take as a proof for this; the verse:

$$ ﴿ قُلِ ٱللَّهُ ثُمَّ ذَرْهُمْ ﴾ $$

"Say: 'Allāh.' Then leave them." [*Sūrah al-Anām* 6:91]

It is wrong to assume the intent in the verse is to suffice in saying only this noun- "Allāh". Reflecting on the beginning of the verse shows the complete and sound intended meaning. Allāh (سُبْحَانَهُ وَتَعَالَى) said:

$$ ﴿ وَمَا قَدَرُوا۟ ٱللَّهَ حَقَّ قَدْرِهِۦٓ إِذْ قَالُوا۟ مَآ أَنزَلَ ٱللَّهُ عَلَىٰ بَشَرٍ مِّن شَىْءٍ قُلْ مَنْ أَنزَلَ ٱلْكِتَٰبَ ٱلَّذِى جَآءَ بِهِۦ مُوسَىٰ نُورًا وَهُدًى لِّلنَّاسِ تَجْعَلُونَهُۥ قَرَاطِيسَ تُبْدُونَهَا وَتُخْفُونَ كَثِيرًا وَعُلِّمْتُم مَّا لَمْ تَعْلَمُوٓا۟ أَنتُمْ وَلَآ ءَابَآؤُكُمْ قُلِ ٱللَّهُ ثُمَّ ذَرْهُمْ ﴾ $$

"They did not account for Allāh the lofty status due to Him when they said: "Nothing did Allāh send down to any human being (by revelation)." Say: "Who then sent down the Book which Mūsā (Moses) brought, a light and a guidance to mankind which you (the Jews) have made into (separate) paper sheets, disclosing (some of it) and concealing much. And you (believers) were taught that which neither you nor your fathers knew." Say: "Allāh (sent it down)." Then leave them." [*Sūrah al-Anām* 6:91]

The correct meaning becomes: "Say Allāh revealed the book of Moses." Therefore, it is a complete sentence; linguistically - a nominal sentence comprised of a subject and predicate. The predicate –"revealed the book."- has been omitted due to its prior referencing. The Arabic language allows such sentence structure.

According to the sources of the legislation, it is disliked to supplicate with only a singular noun. Similar conclusion could be reached logically; a singular noun is not indicative of faith or disbelief, guidance or deviation, or of knowledge or ignorance.

The scholars of the Arabic linguists – surely others – agree that a single noun does not equate a sentence and consequently express any meaningful intent. If anyone were to repeat the noun "Allāh" a thousand times, it will not cause becoming a believer, neither will it grant Allāh's of Paradise. Even the disbelievers make mention of the noun "Allāh" although denying His divinity and/or oneness.

Although Allāh commanded us to make mention of His name and increase His remembrance- such as in:

﴿ فَكُلُواْ مِمَّآ أَمۡسَكۡنَ عَلَيۡكُمۡ وَٱذۡكُرُواْ ٱسۡمَ ٱللَّهِ عَلَيۡهِ ﴾

"So eat of what they catch for you, but pronounce the Name of Allāh over it, and fear Allāh. Verily, Allāh is Swift in reckoning." [*Sūrah al-Mā'idah* 5:4]

﴿ وَلَا تَأۡكُلُواْ مِمَّا لَمۡ يُذۡكَرِ ٱسۡمُ ٱللَّهِ عَلَيۡهِ ﴾

"Eat not (O believers) of that (meat) on which Allāh's Name has not been pronounced (at the time of the slaughtering of the animal)." [*Sūrah al-Anām* 6:121]

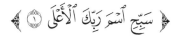

﴿ سَبِّحِ ٱسۡمَ رَبِّكَ ٱلۡأَعۡلَى ۝ ﴾

"Glorify the Name of your Lord, the Most High."
[*Sūrah al-'Alā'* 87:1]

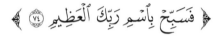

**"Then glorify with praises the Name of your
Lord, the Most Great."** [*Sūrah l-Wāqia'h* 56:74]

It is never the intent to do so by uttering a singular
noun. Instead, the intent is to make mention of the name
in a complete meaningful sense. For example, saying
"glory be to Allāh" or "Praise be to Allāh" and etc.

So, it is affirmed from the above that the invocation of
the singular noun is not legislated. Even more so, the
invocation of only a pronoun. It alone does not indicate
anyone particular; it is dependent on the intent of the
speaker. Sufficing with only the pronoun is farthest
from the *Sunnah*, more delving into innovation, and
more of Shaytān's deception.

In conclusion, the legislated form of supplication is of
complete sentences and meaningful phrases. Such
supplications result in attaining rewards of Allāh,
drawing nearer to Him, an increase of loving Him, and
the likes of lofty pursuits. The fundamental principle of

the religion is to worship Allāh alone in the manner which He legislated."[34]

The above passage contained sufficient clarity leaving no necessity for further elaboration or sense of hesitancy regarding the matter. The truth has been uncovered. However, it is very oddly questionable the insistence of those factions on these deviant forms of supplication-which has no basis in the religion. In return, they abandon the authentic legislated supplications. What compelled them to deter away from the guidance of the Prophet (ﷺ)? Why do they glorify these innovated supplications and belittle the authentic supplications? The supplications that were performed by the most virtuous being and the chief of all mankind-the Prophet (ﷺ).

OUR CALL [35]

[1]: We believe in Allāh and His Names and Attributes, as they were mentioned in the Book of Allāh and the *Sunnah* of the Messenger of Allāh (ﷺ), without *tahrīf* (distortion), nor *ta'wīl* (figurative interpretation), nor *tamthīl* (making a likeness), nor *tashbīh* (resemblance), nor *ta'tīl* (denial).

[2]: We love the Companions (رَضِيَٱللَّهُعَنْهُمْ) of the Messenger of Allāh (صَلَّىٱللَّهُعَلَيْهِوَسَلَّمَ), and we hate those who speak against them. We believe that to speak ill of them is to speak ill of the Religion, because they are the ones who conveyed it to us. And we love the Family of the Prophet (صَلَّىٱللَّهُعَلَيْهِوَسَلَّمَ) with love that is permitted by the *Sharee'ah*. 'Imrān Ibn Husayn (رَحِمَهُٱللَّهُ) said, "O people! Learn the knowledge of the Religion from us, if you do not do so, then you will certainly be misguided." [36]

[3]: We love the People of *Hadīth* and all of the *Salaf* of the *Ummah* from *Ahlus-Sunnah*. Imaam Shātibī (d.790H) – (رَحِمَهُٱللَّهُ) - said, "The *Salafus-Sālih*, the Companions, the

---

[35] Summarized from the biography of Shaykh Muqbil Ibn Hādī al-Wādi'ī with some additions from other sources.

[36] Refer to al-Kifāyah (p. 15) of al-Khatīb al-Baghdādī.

tābi'īn and their successors knew the *Qur'ān*, its sciences, and its meanings the best."[37]

[4]: We despise *'ilmul-kalām* (knowledge of theological rhetoric), and we view it to be from amongst the greatest reasons for the division in the *Ummah*.

[5]: We do not accept anything from the books of *Fiqh* (jurisprudence), nor from the books of *tafsīr* (explanation of the *Qur'ān*), nor from the ancient stories, nor from the *Sīrah* (biography) of the Prophet (ﷺ), except that which has been confirmed from Allāh or from His Messenger (ﷺ). We do not mean that we have rejected them, nor do we claim that we are not in need of them. Rather, we benefit from the discoveries of our Scholars and the jurists and other than them. However, we do not accept a ruling, except with an authentic proof.

[6]: We do not write in our books, nor do we cover in our lessons, nor do we give sermons with anything except the *Qur'ān*, or the authentic and authoritative *hadīth*. And we detest what emanates from many books and admonishers in terms of false stories and weak and fabricated *ahādīth*. 'Abdullaah Ibnul-Mubārak (d.181H)

---

[37] Refer to al-Muwāfiqāt (2/79) of ash-Shātibī.

– (رَحِمَهُ ٱللَّهُ) - said, "The authentic *ahādīth* are sufficient, and the weak *ahādīth* are not needed."[38]

[7]: We do not perform *takfīr* upon any Muslim due to any sin, except *Shirk* with Allāh, or the abandonment of Prayer, or apostasy. We seek refuge in Allāh from that.

[8]: We believe that the *Qur'ān* is the Speech of Allāh, it is not created.

[9]: We hold that our 'obligation is to co-operate with the group that traverses the methodology of the Book and the *Sunnah*, and what the *Salaf* of the *Ummah* were upon; in terms of calling to Allāh the Glorified, and being sincere in worship of Him, and warning from *Shirk*, innovations, and disobedience, and to advise all of the groups that oppose this.'[39] 'So co-operating upon righteousness and piety (*Taqwā*) and mutual advising

---

[38] Refer to al-Jaami' li-Akhlāqir-Rāwī (2/159) of as-Suyootee.

[39] From a *fatwā* by the Committee of Major Scholars dated: 11/16/1417, (no. 18870). It was signed by al-'Allāmah 'Abdul-'Azīz Ibn Bāz, Shaykh 'Abdul-'Azīz Ibn 'Abdullāh aalush-Shaykh, Shaykh 'Abdullāh Ibn 'Abdur-Rahmaan al-Ghudayyaan, Shaykh Bakr Ibn 'Abdullāh Aboo Zayd, and Shaykh Sālih Ibn Fawzaan al-Fawzaan.

necessitates warning against evil and not co-operating with the wicked.'[40]

[10]: We do not deem it correct to revolt against the Muslim rulers as long as they are Muslims, nor do we feel that revolutions bring about reconciliation. Rather, they corrupt the community.

[11]: We hold that this multiplicity of present day parties is a reason for the division of the Muslims and their weakness. So therefore we set about 'freeing the minds from the fetters of blind-following and the darkness of sectarianism and party spirit.'[41]

[12]: We restrict our understanding of the Book of Allāh and of the *Sunnah* of the Messenger of Allāh (صَلَّى اللَّهُ عَلَيْهِ وَسَلَّمَ) to the understanding of the *Salaf* of the *Ummah* from the Scholars of *hadīth*, not the blind-followers of their individuals. Rather, we take the truth from wherever it comes. Moreover, we know that there are those who claim *Salafiyyah*, yet *Salafiyyah* is free from them since they bring to the society what Allāh has prohibited. We believe in 'cultivating the young generation upon this

---

[40] From the words of Shaykh Ibn Bāz in *al-Furqān* magazine (issue no. 14, p. 15).

[41] From *Fiqhul-Wāqi'* (p. 49) of al-Albānī.

Islam, purified from all that we have mentioned, giving to them a correct Islamic education from the start - without any influence from the disbelieving western education.' [42]

[13]: We believe that politics is a part of the Religion, and those who try to separate the Religion from politics are only attempting to destroy the Religion and to spread chaos.

[14]: We believe there will be no honor or victory for the Muslims until they return to the Book of Allāh and the *Sunnah* of the Messenger of Allāh (ﷺ).

[15]: We oppose those who divide the Religion into trivialities and important issues. And we know that this is a destructive *Da'wah*.

[16]: We oppose those who put down the knowledge of the *Sunnah* and say that this is not the time for it. Likewise, we oppose those who put down acting upon the *Sunnah* of the Messenger of Allāh (ﷺ).

[17]: Our *Da'wah* and our *'Aqīdah* is more beloved to us than our selves, our wealth, and our offspring. So we are

---

[42] From *Fiqhul-Wāqi'* (p. 51) of al-Albānī.

not prepared to part with it for gold, nor silver. We say this so that no one may have hope in buying out our *Da'wah*, nor should he think that it is possible for him to purchase it from us for *dīnār* or *dirhām*.

[18]: We love the present day Scholars of the *Sunnah* and hope to benefit from them and regret the passing away of many of them. Imām Mālik said (d.179H) P, "The knowledge of *hadīth* is your flesh and blood, and you will be asked concerning it on the Day of Judgment, so look who you are taking it from."[43]

---

[43] Refer to al-Muhaddithul-Fāsil (p. 416) and al-Kifāyah (p. 21) of al-Khatīb.

Points of Benefit

Page:	Benefit:

Points of Benefit

Page:	Benefit:

Points of Benefit

Page:	Benefit:

Points of Benefit

Page:	Benefit:

Printed in Great Britain
by Amazon